Liz Tresilian lives in the West Country and is the author of several books including ALDANITI, THE STORY OF A CHAMPION and SUN SIGNS FOR CATS.

D0590023

Sun Signs for Dogs

Written and illustrated by
LIZ TRESILIAN

A Futura Book

First published in Great Britain under the title
The Dog Horoscope Book by
Arlington Books, London in 1967

This edition published in 1986
by Futura Publications, a Division of
Macdonald & Co (Publishers) Ltd
London & Sydney

ISBN 0 7088 3019 6

Printed and bound in Great Britain by
Collins, Glasgow

Futura Publications
A Division of
Macdonald & Co (Publishers) Ltd
Maxwell House
74 Worship Street
EC2A 2EN

A BPCC plc Company

Contents

Astrology for Dogs – an Introduction

Too few people realise that astrology gives the caring dog owner a sound basis for ensuring that, firstly, he and his dog will get on and, secondly, that that dog will be at home in the surroundings he has been placed in.

As more and more humans turn to their horoscopes first thing in the morning when their paper arrives to find out about themselves and their families, why should they not also find out about their dogs? After all, the sun gives life to everything on earth – us, the plants and trees, insects, birds – and dogs. There is no good reason why dogs should be left out of all the fun. Especially as astrology is a sure way of getting to know a dog – from the tip of his nose to the end of his tail.

The sun signs, which this book is based upon, are fun. Each of the twelve signs of the zodiac which the sun travels through once a year has its own quirks and foibles, characteristics and behaviour patterns. All of which can be found in dogs – if you know where to look – just as much as in humans. The best – and worst – that can be expected in any dog is revealed in this book.

To get the most out of a dog it is vital that you understand him to the best of your ability, appreciate his whims and peculiarities and then choose him through that understanding – not because you like the colour of his eyes or the way his tail curls. And this is what astrology – through this book – can help you to do. To really get the whole picture you should go to a qualified astrologer with date, time and place of birth and have an individual horoscope charted. But this is not always practical.

Expecting the sun signs to give a complete picture of any

dog suggests that the whole canine population can be divided into twelve neat groups, which is obviously impossible.

As well as the influence of the sun in a dog there is also the moon and eight planets to be taken into consideration. Each dog becomes a mixture of several signs, some featuring more prominently than others. One may be born with his sun in Aries with a strong dash of Pisces and a sprinkling of Gemini, another with his sun in Aquarius with a large spoonful of Taurus and a touch of the Capricorns. On top of which are their own breed characteristics, as well as maternal influences, genetics, pedigree and early environment.

However, there is a lot that can be learnt from the sun signs, and that is where this book starts. The twelve signs of the zodiac can, in fact, reveal a vast amount of information about the behaviour patterns of the dogs born under them: their likely make-up, basic temperament, whether they will be town or country dogs, active or sleepy, who they will get on with, as well as who they will dislike on sight.

The prospective dog owner, having worked out by reading this book which sign appears to produce the pet most compatible with him and best suited to his lifestyle, can still go for a preferred breed or colour – if he is patient enough to wait for a litter or two. The relationship will get off to a much better start than if they had gone out one sunny day and come home with the puppy that smiled at them first.

An understood dog, in surroundings that he will enjoy, with people that he will thrive on, is bound to be a better friend, companion, working animal – whatever – than one who looks, and feels, like a square peg in a round hole: out of step with his environment, permanently underfoot with the people in it.

For the person who already has a dog, whether happily or hating each other, this book can also be a great help. If the birth date is known already they are off with a head start. From there careful study of the book – and the dog – will show which of the other signs are strong in him. Then the happy relationship will really blossom, while the not-so-happy may well be stopped from deteriorating completely.

It is still possible to use the sun signs with dogs whose birth date has got lost in the past. Again careful study of both book and dog should reveal the most likely sign to celebrate their birthday under, if not the actual day, which will not offend the dog at all as he will be pleased with the extra attention and hardly likely to nit-pick. In the case where several signs seem equally probable then go ahead and have a party under each of them; the dog will be thrilled and you will know far more about him than you did before.

Reading this book should enlarge your knowledge and understanding of any dog that you are interested in. For instance, the Capricorn, forever annoying you by jumping onto the dining-room table is not simply being naughty. It is in his nature to get to the top, so he really cannot help himself. He could be tempted to change his habits if he was given his own climbing frame.

The Sagittarian who never sits still, always wandering and causing havoc by having too many friends along the road, sees life as one big adventure put there for his benefit and needs friends as other dogs need bones. He would certainly be more settled if sent on adventure holidays and expeditions.

The Taurean who hates walks and will not set foot in the car simply hates change and will do anything to make sure that he stays put where he knows what's what. He could be soothed and comforted if you sold the car and assured him that you would never go out again!

Having read this book you may be surprised to find that your dog loves music – enjoys gardening – should never have been asked to live in a flat. His inner longings and yearnings may well be a revelation to you – and so might your own!

Aries

March 21 through April 20

The sign of the Warrior or Pioneer
A cardinal fiery sign
Energetic, impulsive, enthusiastic, positive

Ruler: Mars

Harmonious signs: Sagittarius, Leo

Aries

BASIC TEMPERAMENT

ARIES is traditionally the first sign of the Zodiac: the sign of the born-leader—the pioneer of dogs.

A dog born under this sign will be full of vitality, well able to run several packs of hounds right off their feet. But he will have only one aim in life, into which he will channel every drop of excess energy—to get to the front, and to stay there. As he is born under the first sign he must be first dog.

This desire to be in front will be peculiar to the Arian. Early astrologers recognised it and symbolised it by the forward-thrusting horns of the ram. No one since has been able to better this. This is the very essence of the Arian. It is the key to his character; the root of all your troubles.

The way he rushes ahead will drive you mad. He will push between your legs when you get up to put the cat out. He will be out of the house—and sight—before you have taken the lead off its peg, and it will never enter his head to check which way you were going to go. When you go out to the car he will be sitting there waiting for you. He will not take kindly to travelling in the back either.

Watch a group of dogs out on the prowl. The one in front choosing the smells and the tree-trunks will undoubtedly be an Arian. His motto will be 'me first' with no 'please' about it. He will let nothing—I repeat, nothing—stand before him.

LEBENSRAUM

An Arian in a house will be like a fish out of water, never settling properly and finding life with one lot of people in one home inadequate. Do not take offence when he adopts the family next door. It will only be his way of satisfying his need for variety in life and the more he has to occupy him the easier he will be to live with. Forced to make do with just you, he will be bored and dissatisfied; a nagging, discontented dog.

The ideal accommodation for the Arian would be a house the size of Buckingham Palace with surrounding gardens and estates to match. But if like the majority of us you have not a palatial residence to put at the disposal of your dog—a country seat would do at a pinch. The Arian's erratic and demanding manner will soon exhaust you if you are cooped up with him all day. You must live somewhere where you can lose him occasionally. He will get on your nerves in a cottage and if you live in a flat keep the telephone number of Alcoholics Anonymous at the back of your mind.

The Arian will always be on the go from first light until it is too dark for him to see; nervously shifting from one pursuit to another; poking his nose into your private concerns; generally getting under foot. If there is not enough for him to do he will fidget continually and aimlessly. He will never sit still, scratching and biting in a most unbecoming way, very off-putting to the uninitiated. The cause will be self-pity at the monotony of life, not fleas. But a dusting with veterinary powder will not do any harm, and it will always be wise to be on the safe side.

You may be under the happy illusion that your garden is both dogworthy and dogproof. The Arian will prove otherwise. He will stray as naturally as a cat, finding the largest garden a tedious waste of time and he will exhaust the limitations of the average back-of-the-house-patch in a couple of days.

Houdini was an Arian. This may seem rather an extreme example but the ability to find a way out of most places—and situations—will be found to some degree in all Arians. High walls miraculously become stepping stones and fences trip-wires.

And there will always be someone to leave the gate open.

SOCIAL INTEGRATION

The Arian could never be called a 'yes-dog'. Not even by the most optimistic dog-lover. The cold war will begin the minute that his four little puppy legs set foot inside the door. You will both be fighting for the upper hand. You will be desperately trying to assert your right as owner. He will stop at nothing to undermine your position.

The only thing to do will be to work out a plan of campaign at the beginning—and stick to it rigorously. Decide which rules you are going to insist on—and enforce them, overlooking minor matters. This will be compromise. But it will be worth it unless you want a little dictator on your hands, a public menace. A dog who has to be left behind when you go out and shut in the kitchen when you entertain at home.

Even after the most exhaustive training, and here it will be you who will feel the strain, the Arian will still have a mind of his own. There is no need to fear that these hard-hearted methods will cause the dog psychological harm. Just the opposite. He will thrive on it. It will give him something to get his teeth into, which is just what he will appreciate most.

It will take more than a mere human to browbeat an Arian. Persistent correction will leave him untouched. He will take so little notice of it that you will wish that you had bought a goat instead.

One of the most frustrating and disarming characteristics of this dog will be his happy knack of forgetting past failures. Refuse him the last biscuit at tea-time and before you can say 'dog-basket' he will be asking for a piece of cake. You may be driven to ask yourself "Is there any point?" as Sunday after Sunday he demands the best cut off the joint and night after night you have to fight to get anywhere near your own bed.

The Arian will put up with your dicta in a good-humoured way, only losing his temper under extreme provocation, when you deny him what he considers to be his by right. And when he does get cross you will know about it. He will be well able to make his displeasure clear to the person concerned (poor misguided soul) who will be treated to a noteworthy display of back-turning. He will be thoroughly put in his place. The dog will ignore him and go out of its way to be friendly with everyone else, chatting up strangers in the most intimate way;

allowing himself to be picked up and cuddled—normally one of his pet hates; moving up to make room for the cat.

However in the long run this basically warm-hearted animal should prove an amusing—if time consuming—pet, incapable of sulking or bearing a grudge for long. No other type will be capable of such depth of feeling. The Arian will have a lot of affection to give, which he will do whole-heartedly and openly, able to show his approval as obviously as his disapproval.

But this very enthusiasm may lead to trouble. An affectionate, boisterous puppy is one thing. A large, fully grown beast who holds the firm idea that he is a lap-dog, another. Not everyone will appreciate being pinned down to have their ears scrubbed each time they come to see you. So before you lose all your friends you will have to get it across to your dog that there are politer ways for him to show his feelings.

If, despite all this, you are still determined to become an Arian-owned person—go ahead. You never know. You might be the one to make a go of it.

Leo and Sagittarius are the recognised harmonious signs for Aries. People born under them will stand a better chance of pulling it off than others. If anyone is going to achieve the unlikely successful relationship, they should. The stable elements found in both Leonians and Sagittarians will act as a balance to the erratic nature of the Arian. They also have enough of the same energetic and self-expressive qualities to understand each other up to a point.

PERSONAL RELATIONSHIPS

Unfortunately fighting will be second nature to the Arian. He will pick quarrels in a most cantankerous fashion, reading insults into the leg-lifting of the most inoffensive looking creatures. Whether or not aspersions have been cast is something that you will never know, but he will take up the challenge—imaginary or not—before the other dog has time to complete the normal canine civilities.

He will always fight from close quarters, considering slanging matches and circling stiff-legged with his hackles up a waste of time. His idea of sport will be to get in there before his opponent has realised what is happening, and get his teeth well into the skin.

When you do finally manage to separate them your dog may well be covered with blood, so that he looks as if he has not a hope of survival without an immediate transfusion. But it will all wash off and he will not have a scratch on him. The Arian will be good at keeping out of harms way, well able to inflict injury while avoiding actual physical damage to his own person.

AMOROUS INCLINATIONS

When in love the Arian will be a real menace both to you and your neighbours. He will be driven by strong sexual feelings plus the desire to enjoy every situation to the full.

He will be neither tactful nor refined. It will be far better for you if his girl-friends belong to people you have no particular wish to be on good terms with. But just as one dog-owner is getting thoroughly unpleasant and threatening to take action, you will be saved. For the Arian will be fickle, tiring of his girl-friends as he will do of everything else.

Then it will all start again. The telephone calls demanding that you do something about your dog before it gives ideas to the baby; the visits from the police; the irate stranger appearing on your doorstep with a basketful of puppies. With the Arian this will be part of your life. You might even come to miss it when he grows old.

PHYSICAL CHARACTERISTICS

The Arian will be the most active and energetic of all the twelve Zodiacal types. Even a St. Bernard—heavy and lazy as they are when born away from the mountains—will be capable of covering considerable distances without stopping for a nap at every other telegraph pole.

This dog will have a bottomless capacity for exercise: he will lead you up hills; gallop you across plough; drag you through hedges; jump you over walls and trot you on the flat. The more the terrain resembles a never ending assault course the happier he will be.

You will have to accept this and, if necessary, do press-ups before breakfast. If you are not fit enough to keep up with him he will not bother to wait for you, writing you off as a physical wreck who is past his prime and not worth bothering about.

Life in the country will really be the only thing for the Arian (certainly for any of the larger breeds). So if you are unfortunate enough to live in a town where pavements and 'please keep off the grass no dogs allowed' are the orders of the day, and you must have an Arian, try one of the smaller breeds. They will not like it but they will find it easier to accept.

Despite the fact that his impulsive nature will bring him into constant risk of injury, veterinary bills will be low with an Arian. You may think that he is bound to get hurt—even killed—as he charges blindly into the path of an oncoming petrol-tanker. By the time it has skidded to a stop on the pavement he will be well out of the way, laughing.

You may find that this dog will suffer from migraines. Headaches will be common to the Arian but you will be able to cope with them easily enough as they occur. Aspirin and rest in a dark room will do the trick.

In the summer you will have to be more careful. The Arian will catch sunstroke as other dogs catch postmen—easily and frequently. He should not be asked to live in a hot climate and should never be allowed to spend too long in the sun.

JUST YOUR BAD LUCK

If you have picked a primitive Arian he will not be all that different from the run-of-the-mill type—just worse. He will have all the same characteristics but they will be exaggerated, making him much more difficult to deal with.

"Impossible," you may say.

But it isn't.

The primitive Arian will have a complete blank as far as other people are concerned to the extent of refusing to admit that they so much as exist. He will sweep away anyone who happens to be where he wants to be—apparently unaware of their presence. He will be reckless and heedless, deaf and blind to anyone or anything that he has not time for.

A puppy should show which type he is when young, which is something to be thankful for. If you find that you are unfortunate enough to have a primitive Arian on your hands, think twice—perhaps three times—before you let the matter go any further.

Taurus

April 21 through May 21

The sign of the Builder or Producer
A fixed earthy sign
Stubborn, steadfast, systematic, persevering

Ruler: Venus

Harmonious signs: Capricorn, Virgo, Cancer.

Taurus

BASIC TEMPERAMENT

TAURUS is a fixed, earthy sign. The Taurean will be a fixed, earthy dog, uncluttered by complexes and easy to understand. A dog who really will wait to see which way the cat jumps and then make his retreat in the opposite direction.

The most noticeable characteristic of this dog will be his stability of purpose. Of all dogs this one will be the most steadfast and the most dependable. At times he will be the most stubborn; often the most obstinate. He will be a one-track dog, dogged beyond belief. The dog that you will be able to lean against in front of the fire because the effort of getting up and moving away will be greater than that of bearing your weight. The dog that you will not have to teach to sit but to stand, because saving energy will be one of his main preoccupations.

Do not think that life with a Taurean around will be relaxed and soothing. This kind and gentle dog will have his problems which will also become your problems. Admittedly he will be above average for obedience as he will actually prefer to be told what to do. But you will have to watch your step in certain directions.

Above all the Taurean will hate change. He will need a stable background as an agitator needs a cause: without it his life will be pointless. There will be no more doing things on the spur of the moment for you. From the day he arrives you will have to plan all your activities and explain what you are going to do well in advance so that he has time to digest the idea. Then, by the time it happens, he will be prepared and able to cope with the emergency. The impromptu will be unpleasing to the Taurean.

At the back of his mind will be the memory that he has already been uprooted and thrust into the unknown once—when you took him away from his mother. He will be terrified of this happening again. The only way he will have of ensuring against it will be to dig in his roots. He will find a pattern to live by: a routine, that he will then follow single-mindedly.

LEBENSRAUM

Once he has overcome his homesickness the Taurean will quickly adapt his new surroundings to himself, bedding down so firmly that you will soon forget the time when your life was your own; when you could pack up and go away without fear of disapproval; when your day to day life could be as free and unorganised as you pleased and was not controlled by the whims of a dog.

The Taurean will wake, take his morning constitutional, go back to sleep, walk to the garden gate and back, rest, eat his tea, sleep it off, take a look at the stars and finally retire for the night—at the same time every single day. And woe betide you if you do not fall into step with him. This creature of habit will make no allowances for people who like to lie in on Sundays. Seven days a week for fifty-two weeks of the year his routine will never vary.

Unless ... there happens to be a major calamity: an earthquake or the house burning down. Otherwise at any time of the day or night—should you want to—you will know where to find him.

All this may sound rather boring. It will be. There will be times when you feel like putting a bomb under him. But there will also be the time when you find him a blessing—if heavily disguised. When everything goes wrong at once, which can happen in the best run households, the Taurean will be the one dog that you can count on not to chase the cat through the kitchen when the baby has fallen out of its high chair; the vegetables have boiled dry; the sink has blocked and the man has come to paint the stop-cock and you do not know where it is. The dog will not notice that there is anything untoward afoot, least of all add to it in any way. Unless it happens to be time for his meal, of course.

If your circumstances are limited the Taurean will not complain, resigning himself to roughing it quite readily. But he will appreciate luxury being able to see at a glance the sense in wall to wall carpeting throughout the house and he would not say 'no' if you wanted to continue it into the garden. He will wallow in the bliss of your easy chairs, after filling them with cushions, and he will have the palate of a first-class gourmet, ignoring plates of common dog food and your leftovers and eating only the best.

Given the slightest encouragement he will take over your most comfortable piece of furniture to satisfy his belief that possessions mean stability. The special Safari-type-dog-bed that you had sent down from that shop in Knightsbridge will remain empty under the kitchen table.

'His chair,' 'his rug,' 'his fire' will become parts of your conversation and he will guard these prized possessions ferociously, frightening off all but the very strong minded.

The Taurean's link with the earth will give him a practical interest in nature. Within his doggy limitations he will be a keen gardener happy to pick flowers and pull his weight where improving the soil is concerned. He will consider it to be the least he can do in return for his board and lodging—you will

consider it a nuisance, but it will be something you will have to learn to accept.

When he picks one of your prize blooms count ten, put down the riding whip and remember that he was not deliberately trying to upset you and that dog owners have no right to prize blooms in the first place. Do not punish him, try teaching him to pick buttercups instead. Point out their delicate colouring to him and show him how they throw yellow shadows underneath his chin. If that does not work you could try giving him a bone every time he comes in from the garden without a flower. This is not something that you can expect him to learn overnight, but he may catch on if you give him a lot of time.

Impress upon him how clever he is when he digs in the compost heap and you may, though do not count on it, teach him to confine his agricultural pursuits in those parts of the garden that you never have time to get round to, near the dustbins and right down at the bottom.

This tendency to revert to nature will also have less destructive—or constructive, depending on who's opinion it is—ways of showing itself. The highly developed Taurean will find digging and weeding too strenuous and be content to simply commune with nature. He will lie on the grass apparently fast asleep. The occasional flip of his tail, the slight movement of his head as he mouths a foolhardy fly, will be the only signs that he is in fact awake.

SOCIAL INTEGRATION

The Taurean will be naturally obedient and remember what you teach him as a puppy. But when he is older you may run into trouble over incidental matters that did not occur when he was young enough for you to point them out to him.

If there is an extra person staying in the house you may all want to sit down in the evening. Three easy chairs should be enough, counting one for you, one for your husband and one for your guest. You will have forgotten the dog, and four into three does not go. The dog will have to back down. With his feet firmly wedged into the four corners of the chair he will appear glued to it; you will coax him until you are blue in the face, push him from behind and even tip up the chair. Your exertions will merely interrupt his sleep and not disturb him unduly. You will offer your chair to the surprised visitor and make do with a hard one for yourself.

The fact that it is practically impossible to ruffle the Taurean makes him a natural choice for people with small children.

In the same way that he withstood your efforts over the chair his patience will put up with any amount of child-baiting. He will treat finger-poking as a trifling annoyance, tail pulling and riding will be taken in his stride. His most positive reaction will be to heave himself up and amble away.

Capricornians, Virgoans and Cancerians are the most likely people to fit in with a Taurean. They all have the same slightly negative approach to life as a basis for understanding each other. As the Taurean needs to give affection, the sign you are born under will be of less importance than with any of the other types. Once you have won him over he will be yours for life. A dog who will stick by you through rebuff and neglect, as steadfast in this respect as in any other.

PERSONAL RELATIONSHIPS

On the whole the Taurean will be a peaceful creature, taking to dogs as easily as he does humans. But when he does come across a disrespectful member of his own kind he will rise to the occasion valiantly in unflinching attack. This will be the exception rather than the rule. He will prefer to avoid conflict instead of expending the energy that is bound to be wasted if it does come to a fight.

AMOROUS INCLINATIONS

In love the male Taurean will keep to his general characteristics. Once attracted to another dog he will stay that way, immune to the charms of others. There will be a lot of the earthy element in him which will make him refuse to accept love at a distance. He will crave for the constant physical presence of the bitch, allowing nothing short of the Pacific Ocean to separate them. However, the Taurean will be as averse to exercise as he is to change and if you want to make life easier for yourself you might buy another dog in the hope that having his romance on the doorstep will stop him from looking elsewhere.

It would then be on your doorstep too and you will be without upset neighbours and early morning trips to fetch him home.

PHYSICAL CHARACTERISTICS

Whoever it was who thought of the bull as a symbol for the Taurean must have been a genius. Not only are the Taurean and the bull alike mentally, both being possessive and brave, but also physically. They are both powerfully built, especially around the head and neck.

The Taurean will be without exception a big dog. Even one of the miniature breeds will be gross compared to its fellows; a point worth remembering if you want your dog to suffer the indignities of the show ring. The judges would take one look at a Taurean Toy-Poodle or miniature Dachshund—and that would be that. You would be relegated to the back row, and there you would stay.

But with a Boxer or Bull-Dog it would be another matter altogether. His massive jaws and grotesque neck would be bound to bring you success, and the dog would enjoy eating the rosette afterwards.

The female Taurean will be near enough to nature to make the perfect mother. She will not only be able to cope with the whole operation from start to finish, she will actually like it. Natural childbirth will not be in it as she shepherds her large litter into the world with the ease of one who has been doing just that for the whole of her life. You will simply have to take a back seat. The only chore that will be left to you will be to find the puppies homes—which is beyond the scope of any dog.

The Taurean's natural largeness will have to be very carefully watched or, with very little effort it will become overweight, which is not the same thing at all. If left to his own devices the Taurean would eat himself into an early grave. It will be up to you to restrict his maximum intake each day if you want to avoid the unpleasant job of suddenly presenting him with a reducing diet when he is older. He would not appreciate this at all and life would be intolerable. You would be well aware that you were not doing it for fun while the dog would be convinced that you were doing it to satisfy your sadistic nature.

You will have to decide exactly how much food he can have, following your own reasoning, not the dog's. It will be the only way: no tit-bits at meals, no sweets between meals, one meal a day and one biscuit only when he goes to bed. He will stand a better chance of understanding what you are trying to do if you follow a similar plan for yourself. Only do be careful not to let him catch you filling up on roast chicken when you think he is safely playing in the garden.

The Taurean will be inclined to suffer from ear disorders. It may take the form of everyday earache but a Taurean Spaniel will have more evil-smelling ears than you had imagined could be possible. It will be unpleasant to have him in the same room as yourself, let alone the house. And as it will never be easy to relegate the Taurean to the nether regions you will have to take drastic action at the first sniff of trouble. Professional treatment will be the only hope you have of coming to terms with this complaint.

JUST YOUR BAD LUCK

At his most primitive the Taurean will be a bore. There is no other word to describe him. The dog will be dead from the neck up and tedious beyond compare. He will be stodgy and grasping; lazy and indolent, and self-indulgent. He will be slavishly glued to routine and mulishly obstinate.

Physical activity will be beyond him. If you want to get him somewhere you will have to carry him and humping a fully grown, primitive Taurean around will be no mean feat. This inactive life will be his downfall. He will store up too much energy for a rainy day that never comes, and grow morbid and morose which will result in his sudden, and often early, death.

If you do not want this to happen—some people do manage to work up quite an affection for the primitive Taurean—you will have to find a way of getting him to his feet. It will not be easy, but it has been done.

Gemini

May 22 to June 21

The sign of the Inventor
A mutable airy sign
Restless, clever, exuberant, expressive

Ruler: Mercury

Harmonious signs: Aquarius, Libra

Gemini

BASIC TEMPERAMENT

GEMINI is the first of the double signs, signifying a duplicity of character in those born under it. It is ruled by Mercury and in the Geminian you will find all the qualities attributed to that person.

This dog will be restless, exuberant, versatile, and a lot of other things besides, at one and the same time. A match for the average human even when on his best behaviour.

His aim in life will be to find as many outlets as possible for both sides of his nature, to enable full expression of his unusually high intelligence quota. And this need for change—or craving for diversity—will be apparent from the time his eyes take their first bleary look at the world and he realises that he has been in the same place with the same companions for nearly a fortnight. He will try to rectify this by throwing himself at whatever is there to keep him in, in vain because he will still be very small. Then he will bring to mind the well worn saying that if Mahomed can not go to the mountain the mountain must come to Mahomed and proceed to squeal until a new face, yours—rushing to see which of your little puppies has broken its neck—appears to brighten his outlook.

His first battle will have been won, and although he will tire of looking at you as quickly as you tire of listening to him, he will never forget it. From that day on he will never fail to get the variety so necessary to his existence, albeit they will in their turn be rejected with a consistency that may surprise you in such an inconsistent animal.

His diversity of purpose will be most noticeable while he is still young: it will be very noticeable when he is ageing, for the Geminian has also been blessed with everlasting youth and will never grow up. It will be obvious through his extended second puppyhood, and has been known to reach as far as the seventh or eighth.

This dog will be the eternal puppy—with a split personality.

LEBENSRAUM

The arrival of a Geminian puppy into a well-organised household will be bound to result in chaos, if not at first, as soon as the novelty of his surroundings has worn off. At the very beginning everything will be new to him satisfying his curiosity in a way that was never found for the elephant's child. The house, its contents and the people in it will give him more than food for thought.

The length of this Indian summer will depend entirely on the size of house you are offering to your dog, how varied its make up and how large a family you have. Once he knows what grows under the beds; that your slippers taste of felt and fluff; that he can turn six somersaults between the half-landing and the groundfloor, and that you make do with only three complete changes of winter underwear, and reaches the stage of climbing up the curtains to see who lives behind the pelmet, you will know that your job of keeping him amused has just begun.

A constant supply of unboiled socks, cigarette packets—preferably complete with cigarettes—hearth brushes, feather dusters and sacks of coal will keep him occupied, for a while. But, as with all intelligent dogs, the time will come when he feels the need for some form of amusement that will present more of a challenge: something that he can really get his teeth into, like learning to read.

Regular trips to the library to explain away the torn-up remains of what was once their property may grow tedious. It will certainly prove to be expensive. You could make him take them back and do the explaining, or you could change your branch in search of a dog-owning librarian. Or you could teach him that newspapers are also readable and not nearly so costly and make more mess. You will probably find that the easiest way out is prevention, by removing all books from the house and locking them away in the garage roof.

The only time that you will be a hundred per cent sure of this dog's whereabouts will be when he is firmly attached to you by a lead. Then there will only be one place for him, at the end of it. The rest of the time he will never be where you think he is or doing what you think he is doing. Keeping you guessing will be a favourite game to the Geminian, as he bewilders you by turning up out of the blue when you least expect him, or disappears completely.

Beyond doing your utmost to keep life interesting for him, there is very little you can do. Moving house, admittedly drastic, is something you may be driven to in desperation, because the Geminian would like to do this as other people change their sheets. You could try buying a healthy female cat in the hope that the constant stream of changing faces will keep his mind off the monotony of life. But even that will pall eventually.

SOCIAL INTEGRATION

The natural charm of the Geminian will make him so easy to get on with that in no time at all he will have the whole family twisted right round his dew-claw. Because at heart he will be a giver, bent on improving the state of those around him.

It has been said of this type of dog that his real purpose in life

is simply to make it more interesting and more beautiful for those he loves. And that only when he has achieved this will he be happy. It will certainly be interesting to watch him at work, providing that you are not the object of his attentions. The way that he will choose to go about this will be governed by his surroundings. You need not expect a dog who lives in a third-floor flat to start bothering with flower arrangements. But beauty is in the eye of the beholder so you need not expect a country dog to bother with such trivialities when his idea of beauty may be a bone, lovingly resurrected from a sojourn with the worms and presented to you dramatically in the middle of a tea party. It may be a carpet strewn with the fish paper and a couple of stockings thrown in for added effect, or it may be a room full of dogs carefully selected from the back streets and rubbish dumps, because you are so obviously a person who adores stray animals.

Whatever form it takes it will be his way of showing you how much he wants to please, and it will continue until you register a satisfactory amount of pleasure and delight.

This need for understanding and appreciation from his owner will also show in the readiness with which he will accept your teaching him to sit, lie or come to heel. Providing you do not try anything that could be degrading to a dog, like jumping through a hoop or pushing a wheel-barrow round the living room, for the Geminian will never bother to learn anything that he does not find congenial. It will also show in his complete inability to suffer alone or in silence. When unhappy or in pain it will be impossible for the Geminian to keep it to himself. Relief will only come when he has made everybody else thoroughly uncomfortable, then, having passed the buck— or whatever it was—he will relax, while you spend the rest of the night shaking your pillows and making cups of tea.

Leonians will have strong enough personalities to make the right decision when the Geminian is torn between two equally attractive possibilities, and there will be enough sympathy between the two to ensure compatibility. The broad-minded Aquarian will also find life easy with the Geminian, but no Taurean should ever consider this type for a pet. A house containing these two together will be a case of man eats dog and dog eats man.

PERSONAL RELATIONSHIPS

The Geminian will never be more unpredictable than when he is with other dogs. His quickly changing moods will be reminiscent of the Sparrow, his need for fresh faces and smells—the common flea; both of which are believed to come heavily under the influence of Gemini.

While he is in the middle of a group of dogs holding their attention, he will be friendly, but let one dog step out of line by taking his stick, and he will be ready for a fight. He will bite the innocent offender and then hastily retire to a safe distance to watch the outcome of his action. Should the rival decide to answer back and make a fight of it, he will be completely put out and burst into tears. This will disarm almost any dog, and with his stick back once again, he will be the picture of a dog who loves his fellow creatures and has never heard of a vicious streak.

AMOROUS INCLINATIONS

The Geminian will be as two faced in love as he is in everything else, having as many girl friends as other dogs have hot dinners. He will also be an inverted snob, actually preferring bitches that have come from homes where pedigrees have not been heard of and good breeding is a naughty word. Providing they can offer him the response and affection that he so badly needs, he will never look higher than these sweepings of the dog world.

Mongrels, whatever their shape, size, colour or parentage, will appear as beautiful to the sex hungry Geminian as Venus did to Velazquez. And however this may annoy the owner of a well-bred dog he will never be able to say that the results were not interesting.

PHYSICAL CHARACTERISTICS

You will always be able to recognise the Geminian by the speed with which he darts from pillar to post and back again. He will be slightly underweight, alert and graceful.

His nervous energy will carry him through any amount of all day hikes, cat chases and races with motor-cycles. It will fail him the minute that you suggest he goes down to fetch the papers or accompanies Granny on her afternoon walk; anything uncongenial will bring on an attack of nervous exhaustion in the form of complete collapse, with the dog unable to do so much as lift his own tail.

In time you will come to recognise the warning signs of these bouts of indisposition. The vacant expression, the drooping eyelids and sagging knees will tell you that it is time for you to assert your authority and regain control of the situation by changing the subject.

Like all puppies, a well-balanced diet, plenty of fresh air and sleep at regular times will keep the Geminian healthy . . . apart from knock-knees, a weakness peculiar to this type which you will be able to do nothing about.

JUST YOUR BAD LUCK

The primitive Geminian will be born a thief and stay that way. He will take food, sympathy and other peoples' belongings with a determination that no canine reformatory would be able to cure. But most of all it will be his draining of your affection that will be difficult to accept, because he will be unable to give any in return. When you grow tired of lavishing attention on a dog that does nothing to earn it, and begin to ignore him, he will get in your way and steal from beneath your nose so that you have no way of avoiding him.

This unrewarding dog is very rare; usually he will be an exaggerated version of the evolved type, more inconsistent, more unreliable and completely unable to make up his mind over quite ordinary matters such as whether to play indoors or out, or whether to eat his dinner or leave it. No sooner have you shut the door on him because he asked to be let out than he will be on the wrong side of it, barking to come in again. Revolving doors?

Cancer

June 22 to July 22

The sign of the Teacher or Lunatic
A cardinal watery sign
Tenacious, patient, sensitive, motherly, changeable

Ruler: the Moon

Harmonious signs: Pisces, Scorpio, Taurus

Cancer

BASIC TEMPERAMENT

CANCER is a contrary sign having a close affinity with the sea and the tides. The dog born under it will be an up and down sort of dog with a determination to stay put.

Patience will be his most noticeable characteristic and he will be extremely tenacious. Once he has fastened his teeth into something that he wants—an article of clothing or the bathmat —he will do his best to hang on to it. But unlike the crab, he will not be able to shed a limb and grow another one overnight and it will take him some time to learn that if he does hold onto something so firmly that he loses two or three teeth they will not be instantly replaced. As false teeth are hard to come by for a dog, the easiest way out will be to give in to him occasionally.

The Cancerian will appear superficially to be a timid, sensitive dog, retiring and quite content to be left unnoticed.

Although he will treat all unknown objects, whether they be animal, vegetable or mineral, with extreme caution he will only be doing it for effect. When he hides behind the sofa rather than be exposed to a large paper bag or breaks into uncontrollable shivers at the sight of a new washing-up bowl he will be out to get attention which he will love more than anything else.

Because he will be prone to every emotion known to dogs he will be moodier than most. Joy, sorrow, anger, horror and despair will overcome him with deep intensity so that they become too much for him to bear alone. When he cries you will cry, when he is happy you will run round the room chasing your tail and when he is frightened you will be terrified. But never laugh at the Cancerian when he is in trouble: he may forgive, but he will never forget.

LEBENSRAUM

The Cancerian will arrive in your house with the intention of settling down and making the best of it. It will be the place that he has chosen—for it will not be within his capabilities to realise that it was really you who chose him—in which he intends to live out his life. He will build up security for himself along the lines of squatters rights. He will start by beating the bounds of his new domain and then further establish himself by penetrating every corner so that those who come after him will be left in no doubt as to somebody having been there before them.

Once this stage is over and the property is his he will see to his more trival comforts, ensuring that his day to day life leaves nothing to be desired. He will collect from the house and garden any objects that took his fancy when he was making his preliminary inspection. Rugs, hot water bottles, the odd shoe and even an old hat will all be assembled in and around his bed.

Having bought his house and then furnished it he will guard his 'possessions' with more care than a mother for an only child. He will sit on as many as possible for as much time as possible visibly regretting any time that he has to spend out of their sight. If you do manage to take some of them away when he is not looking, he will notice that they are missing and not rest until he has sought them out and restored them to their correct place. No amount of persuasion will make him waver

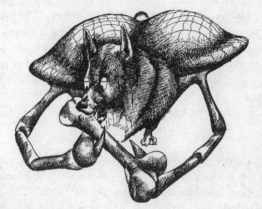

from his belief that possession is nine-tenths of the law and that you should not have been so careless as to leave it lying about in the first place.

There will be another side to the Cancerian, and although it will not show until he is older, it will be well worth your while to take into consideration from the start. He will be moonstruck, as heavily influenced by lunar powers as the sea and the waves.

When you buy your Cancerian you should buy a calendar as well; one that gives the stages of the moon in detail, especially the dates of the full moon. This will be the time when you will have trouble. When the moon is at its peak the Cancerian will behave more oddly than a medium who has worked himself into a trance. He will wail, cavort and howl to the moon to show that he recognises how important it is to his life.

As this will only happen at night his vocal arrangements will not endear you to your neighbours. You will be able to sleep through it using ear-plugs, but they will be subjected to the full horror of having their sleep interrupted by someone else's dog. Windows will fly up, rude words will echo through the night and the telephone will ring until you, too, get out of bed and do something about it.

The only way to avoid this will be to keep him in the dark on his first and every following full moon. Fetch him in early and draw all the curtains, and do not let him out again until the morning, however urgent he may say it is. In this way he should never see the moon in its exciting state, and will not fully understand what it is that makes him restless, irritable, and more than a little nervous.

SOCIAL INTEGRATION

This is where the Cancerian will come into his own. He will be affectionate and loyal, and faithful whatever you subject him to. Put him in kennels while you go off and enjoy yourselves, and when you return home he will welcome you as if the situation had been reversed and it was he who swam and sunbathed while you lay in all the misery of abandonment, unloved and uncared for in a shed at the back of some stranger's house. No separation however long will make him forget the person to whom he belongs, which makes the Cancerian the most likely dog to survive the stringent quarantine regulations imposed in this country. A six-months stretch will be nothing to this type once he is back with his family.

Like all born teachers the Cancerian knows that he will have to learn first, and he will lap up all that you want to teach him, and even ask for more. This he will accept until he reaches the age of being able to think for himself when he will bring it all up again, take stock of it and reject anything that he does not consider to be necessary. So while you may have a puppy that sits on command and comes when you call him it will not always follow that he will grow up to be as well behaved. By the time he is a year old he may have decided that it is purely his concern when and where he sits himself, and nothing at all to do with you. He will never forget anything that you have taught him and should you want to change something that you insisted on when he was young he will invariably hang on to it as the only worthwhile lesson that you did subject him to.

If you encourage the Cancerian puppy to sleep curled up on your bed because he is too irresistible to leave in the cold kitchen overnight, he will grow up knowing that this is what a good dog should do even though you take up so much room that there is not enough for him to stretch out comfortably, and no amount of re-schooling will make him think otherwise. Should you spend time on the novelty of teaching your dog to retrieve a ball, he will grow up with the firm idea that whenever you throw anything out you want it brought back. Dustbins will be emptied and bread you put out for the birds will be placed at your feet with the dedication of a really obedient dog.

Having studied hard when he was young, the older Cancerian will want to pass on his knowledge without paying much attention to the methods he uses as long as he gets his message across. It will not take him long to have his owners in complete understanding of his wishes and fulfilling them as and when he sees fit. When he wants you to sit, you will, even if he has to knock against the back of your knees. When he wants you to get up in the night, you will because he will make so much noise that you will be afraid of the neighbours ringing up the R.S.P.C.A. If he wants you to change his diet, you will, if only to save yourself the trouble of clearing up after him each time he brings up a meal that was not to his liking. You will never be in doubt when there is anything that you can do for him and you will probably be amazed at the speed with which you obey him. You may think that next time he can wait or do without; but it will be just the same and he won't.

Discipline will be difficult between you and this dog. You will have to be very careful to avoid appearing sympathetic. Never chastise him when he is trying to help you however unhelpful he has been or his suffering will be quite out of proportion to the crime committed. The form of discipline you finally select will be a personal matter between the two of you. Severity will probably be useless as it may damage his sensitive nature and make him morbid so that he becomes wilful, doing what he pleases when he pleases. Coercion will be meaningless to him while force may succeed for a little while. Either way, sooner or later the dog will take a dim view and follow his own inclinations.

Pisceans and Scorpionians will make the best owners for the Cancerian. The Piscean will be receptive and impressionable and well suited to put up with the whims that will be part of this dog. But as the Cancerian is basically loving he will go out of his way to understand anyone, except Sagittarians . . . fire and water do not mix.

PERSONAL RELATIONSHIPS

Providing you leave the Cancerian to make his own canine friends he will be an amenable dog. But he will insist on choosing for himself and reject any 'nice' dogs you present to him on grounds that you will not be able to argue with as you will not know what they are.

He will have a large circle of friends, all hand picked, and he will like to spend a certain amount of his time in their company. Playing in a garden by himself will seem dull to a dog who knows that if he can just get through the gate there will be plenty to do and a lot to talk about. As often as he can he will be off down the street leaving his visiting cards with friends who are out and getting up to mischief with those that are around.

The only dogs that he will come to blows with will be those that are forced upon him. Dogs that come to stay with friends of yours; dogs at houses you take him to visit and the dog that you offer to look after while its owners are on holiday. All dogs that he could perfectly well do without and does not see why he should be polite to. The rest of the time he will be peaceful enough, ignoring dogs that he has not got time for and are not thrust upon him.

AMOROUS INCLINATIONS

At first the Cancerian will be too shy to betray his feelings for a member of the opposite sex in case they are not returned. But as he grows older his feelings will be so intense once they have been wakened that he will no longer be able to control them. So although his love life will start with a trail of unhappy affairs, unrequited love and love at a distance, it will steadily improve until he has one of the worst reputations in the area.

A complete disinterest in anything—food, walks and toys— while your dog skulks about the house hiding his head in dark corners will be the indications that he is suffering the first stage. Then his complete disappearance as he treats your house like a one-star hotel will tell you that he has at last grown more confident and found his feet.

As long as you treat his affairs as nothing out of the ordinary and never laugh at them, the Cancerian will not be afraid to bring his girl friends home so that you can look them over and know exactly what he is up to, even if there is nothing that you can do about it. He will be as faithful in love as he is in all his other relationships and he will be extremely tenacious should anyone be so unwise as try to separate him from a bitch. The results could be damaging to him for the rest of his life.

Unlike other dogs the Cancerian will take an interest in his offspring—a fatherly interest—and if any of them find homes within his reach he will consider it his duty to visit them and occasionally bring them home. What else can a parent do who is forced to live apart from his family?

PHYSICAL CHARACTERISTICS

The Cancerian will be a boney specimen and any bulk he does manage to accumulate will be confined to the shoulders. His legs will be long compared to the rest of his body. This peculiar formation means that very few Cancerians will be true to their breed, unless you cross a Bull Dog with an Afghan when the long legs and heavy shoulders will cancel each other out. The only other point against the appearance of this type of dog will be his walk, a sort of shifting, sideways movement which makes it impossible for him to go anywhere in a straight line.

The emotional side of this dog will be stronger than the physical. Misunderstandings will cause complete breakdowns, emotional in reason and physical in practice. Your efforts to get him on his feet again will be useless until he is ready, because he will enjoy wallowing in his own misery and will make the most of every opportunity.

The Cancerian bitch will have a strong sense for the responsibilities of motherhood, should she be given the chance, and will not make it easy for you when the time comes to take the puppies away from her. There will always be some excuse for letting them stay with her another night, and she usually manages to make so much fuss over the idea of losing the whole litter, that you end up with another dog determined to get as much as he can out of the family budget.

A short life span is all that can be expected with this type. The few that do survive to old age will become increasingly difficult to handle with each additional year. Their emotional lapses will cause so much trouble, especially with the male, that you will be led to doubt their sanity.

JUST YOUR BAD LUCK

The primitive Cancerian will be a slave to all the moods that afflict him. Every emotion he suffers will be exaggerated by his over powerful imagination. He will make up situations to stimulate himself if life is too normal to produce them for him, using your reactions to gauge his success. Burying a bone and accusing you of taking it and hiding it from him will be nothing compared to the show of misery he will put on if you go and leave him for five minutes when all the time he was quite happy unpicking your embroidery.

When actual physical damage does occur this dog will eat out on it for the rest of his life. A thorn in his foot when he was a puppy will still cause him acute pain after his hair has begun to turn grey. The foot will be waved at you because pressure is bad for it and you do not understand. You could try asking the vet to remove the whole foot, otherwise you will have to get used to the sympathy he will get from other people who will look on you as being extremely hard-hearted to expect such a lame dog to carry home the shopping.

When he is really ill he will ignore you for weeks on end, which will be a relief, until he suddenly changes his mind and once again returns to life with more fictitious demands upon your generous nature.

Leo

July 23 to August 23

The sign of the King or President
A fixed fiery sign
Proud, energetic, domineering, authoritative

Ruler: the Sun

Harmonious signs: Sagittarius, Aries.

Leo

BASIC TEMPERAMENT

LEO is the sign of the ruler or commander—the veritable King of Dogs. Or so the dog born under it would like you to believe.

This dog will be regal in his bearing, commanding in his presence. He will be self-controlled and ambitious and, above all, domineering. His attitude to life will be that of a supreme being who sees himself as separate from the lesser species with whom he unfortunately cannot avoid coming into contac during day-to-day life. He will expect this attitude to be subscribed to and respected, and the funny thing is that it will be. Throughout his life doors will be held for him to walk through, windows shut when there is a draught, objects moved out of his way and his every whim pandered to immediately he makes it known.

This is because the Leonian will be gifted in the art of getting people to do things for him, so subtly that they will never know they have in fact been got at. His powers of persuasion will be such that you will really believe, when you stop the car and get into the back seat to make room for him in the front, that it was your idea. His pretence at being sick will have been so realistic as to leave no room for the idea that he might have been acting. The slurps and suckings from behind you will have sounded so genuine that you will give up your seat readily, rather than have the job of clearing it all up afterwards.

This will be a bossy dog who will rule all that he surveys with a tail of hair, if left to his own devices.

LEBENSRAUM

In the same way that an Englishman considers his home to be his castle, the Leonian will consider your home to be his palace and a considerable amount of his powers of organisation will be directed at turning it into a suitable background for a dog of his standing. He will select a room for himself, which will be pointed out to you so that you know exactly where you stand, and then he will see that the fittings and furnishings are up to scratch. Lesser matters such as your own domestic arrangements will then be left to you to take care of.

He will hold court in his palace receiving all the neighbourhood dogs as his subjects—it will not be for you to say 'no dogs allowed'—and it will be here that he makes his plans for the running of his kingdom. Buckets of water left ready by the window over the front door will prove a useful deterrent if carefully aimed, or you could stand by the gate all day with an air gun refusing admittance on pain of a very sore behind.

The Leonian will retaliate by telling his ministers where the backdoor is, for he will never be driven to find another place to receive his endless stream of petitioners.

It will also be from his palace that the Leonian will make his sorties into the outside world—his royal tours. While he is on these trips will be the time for you to tighten your defences; check the rabbit wire that surrounds the garden to make sure that it is still dog-proof; refill the water buckets on the landing and lay aniseed trails away from your gate.

A house that is open house to all the dogs in the area whatever their background or thoughts on personal hygiene may be a very exhausting place to live in. You will have to be prepared to spend a lot of time wiping up in dark corners and spraying your furniture with the latest insecticides. This will be the penalty—and the lot—of the proud owner of a Leonian dog.

SOCIAL INTEGRATION

The Leonian would rather not integrate at all and will only do so if put firmly in his place when he is a puppy. And put in the place that you consider to be his, not the one he thinks is right for himself.

When the Leonian puppy first commands you to remove his box from the pantry to the spare-bedroom explain to him very kindly that he will have to make do where he is, and shut the door on him. You will have to steel yourself to his cries and moans . . . unless you want to be in the position of having to crave an audience with your dog each time you want to put him out.

You will have to explain to him that of course he is important to you, probably your favourite dog, but he is not necessarily all important. That he can do what he is meant to do before you go to bed because you are not going to rush down stairs throughout the night each time he feels that he cannot keep his legs crossed any longer. You will also have to impress upon him somehow that a dog who barks noisily for his meals will get nothing while a dog who sits quietly and does not

bother anyone will get regular prompt service. Setting him a good example will teach him more quickly than any other way, even if you do feel a bit ridiculous at the time.

Having overcome these small problems, you will find the Leonian a very charming and rewarding dog, easier to live with than he sounds at first because of one exceptional quality: a deep faith in humanity. He will believe that everyone does really want to do their best for him and think all the more of them for it. He will be very appreciative when you pull yourself out of a chair to take him for a walk at a time when it is the last thing that you feel like doing. He will not mind at all that you are doing it to stop him tying your feet up with the lead which he managed to fetch from behind the kitchen door.

He will never ask too much of one person for with his powers of leadership and organisation he will also have a strong sense of delegation knowing instinctively that he would get nothing at all if he expected one person to be able to take care of all his requirements. So while one member of the family is appointed Minister of Food and Water, another will be Minister of Exercise, another of Health and Hygiene, and so on until he has used up all the available help.

Generally the Leonian will be able to adapt any Zodical type to living with him, but he will find Sagittarians and Arians less trouble than the others. The Sagittarian because he will be happy and optimistic enough not to feel squashed by the Leonian and the Arian because this type will always go its own way and will never get the feeling that he is being put upon by a domineering dog.

Whatever type you are, providing you can prove your ability to look after the Leonian, he will be a loyal and affectionate dog. So much so that were you ever attacked or threatened by anything he would endanger himself rather than see you hurt.

PERSONAL RELATIONSHIPS

The Leonian will expect to have influence over dogs in very much the same way that he does over humans, but he will be more belligerent through not having the same faith in his own kind as he does in people. With a Leonian in the street or village the majority of the dogs will work together, doing what he has told them to do, accepting the most insulting behaviour from him as his right.

Any dog who happens to find himself excluded from this circle would do best to ask his people to move away from the district. You will never be able to pin any blame on the Leonian for causing other dogs to suffer and be afraid of walking the streets in ones, for he will never be seen fighting, that would be too far beneath him. In fact your neighbours will often congratulate you on his peaceful nature when they have to pull their own dogs out of battles. They will not know, as you will, that it was your dog who put theirs up to it.

When he decides that the time has come for another dog to be taught a lesson he will leave the house quite calmly, picking up his followers at pre-arranged lamp posts as he makes his way to the battlefield. These dogs will then be neatly deployed in strategic positions for ambush, while he takes himself to a safe vantage point to watch the arrival of the unsuspecting prey. When this dog has been savaged and left with his tail between his legs, the Leonian will return home as quietly as he left, safe in the knowledge that he neither drew blood himself, nor put his royal personage in any physical danger.

Only when faced with insolent insubordination will he fight himself, and then only if he is alone and has no one to do it for him. He will use a curt and insensitive form of attack which will be forceful enough to do the most damage in the least amount of time.

AMOROUS INCLINATIONS

Through an over-generous nature towards members of the opposite sex the Leonian will have widespread and often misplaced affections. He will consider himself entitled to the favours of all the bitches within his area, which will keep him fully occupied. He will have enough energy to be able to pursue one bitch in the morning, another in the afternoon and yet another in the evening, all in different directions and living quite a long way apart.

When denied the object of his attentions his emotions will be passionate and uncontrolled, often verging on the unreasonable. He will not see why this should be done to him. No kennel will keep him out for long. Nor will anti-mate put him off the scent.

PHYSICAL CHARACTERISTICS

The Leonian will have a well-proportioned body, slender limbs and a graceful walk. He will be the perfect specimen of whatever breed he belongs to, the champion of his class. The ideal dog for those who enjoy the paraphernalia of the show ring.

Apart from the fact that the judges will automatically be impressed by his air of superiority and handsome appearance, the other dogs in the ring will have gathered that there is a Leonian among them. They will know that if they find themselves placed above him he will give them immediate retribution when they are back on their benches. This would be one of the rare occasions when the Leonian would be so angry that he would fight his own battles, and no dog could be expected to bring that on himself however much he would reduce his stud-fee by losing the championship. The other dogs will put on an act to convince the judges that they are poor unspirited creatures, second rate and not worthy of consideration. They will hang their heads, scuffle their feet and clamp their tails between their legs. The dressing down they will get from their owners afterwards will be nothing compared to the wrath off the Leonian.

The average Leonian will have a constitution as strong as his mind and if he does suffer at all it will be from back trouble. This dog will always be prone to weakness in his spine, if not slipped discs it will be the vertebrae joining together, so he should never be expected to sleep in a draught, lift heavy objects, jump up and down or even think heavy thoughts if it can possibly be avoided. He will go along happily with these precautions, much preferring to sleep in the warm and have all the harder things done for him.

JUST YOUR BAD LUCK

The primitive Leonian will be afflicted with an even more inflated sense of his own importance. He will assume airs and graces that can only be called ridiculous when found in a dog and lord it over his inferiors, you, and anyone else who happens to be around.

He will only become attached to people who are prepared to play up to his importance, stroke him the right way and he will never, ever, put himself out for anybody, which will be exceedingly tedious when you use up syphon upon syphon of soda water to neutralise his acid and have to take three daily papers instead of one just to keep a supply of newspaper to hand.

His first need will be a comfortable 'throne' from which he can survey the scene and supervise behaviour in the home. The more well cushioned it is and the more costly the covers, the better, so it will probably be your very best chair. Once ensconced in it he will either fidget until he has torn up the cushions and wrecked the fabric, or snooze loudly, his royal snore shaking the house from top to bottom.

The only person who stands a chance of gaining his affection will be someone who is weak-willed enough to kowtow and pay homage. Someone who will be happy to sit beside him paring his nails and combing his coat; someone who has nothing better to do than spend all their time pandering to a dog.

He will be able to swallow flattery until you would expect it to stick in the back of his throat, only it never will. He will be a dog who is in perpetual fear of having his throne swept from beneath him without ever realising that he is far more likely to be swept off the top of it by an irate hand.

Virgo

August 24 to September 23

The sign of the Critic
A Mutable earthy sign
Exact, methodical, discriminating, intelligent

Ruler: Mercury

Harmonious signs: Capricorn, Taurus

Virgo

BASIC TEMPERAMENT

THIS mutable earthy sign is linked to all the fruits of the earth, especially all domesticated animals. Through this influence the Virgoan will be more resigned than any other type to the role assigned to him. To him the correct position in life will be that of the pet.

This dog will relax under authority, even expand, finding it natural to do what he is told rather than follow his own inclinations which he will know to be inferior. Placed in a house to live among humans and give them pleasure he will strive towards becoming the perfect pet; the Virgin symbolising perfection of character rather than the single state, although a few of them will be chaste as well.

He will sit beside you, on the floor of course for where else is a dog's place? If he is small his head will rest upon your foot; if large, upon your knee. His gaze will be raised to you in unquestioning admiration, his eyes paying homage to your superiority. At least, that is what he will look like, but beneath the surface things will be very different. Never think that this dog will be subservient to the extent of over shadowing himself or so willing to please that he will be shallow and uninteresting. The Virgoan will have a mind of his own, a formidable one. He will simply be better equipped than other dogs to accept human foibles, seeing them as unavoidable nuisances from which he will gain strength of character.

All the time that he is flattering you his mind will be working hard on yours to offer him a more comfortable seat—your lap —so that he does not have to give a bad impression by taking it without being invited.

The Virgoan will be as sensitive to discomfort as the Princess was to the pea.

LEBENSRAUM

Beyond stocking up with the usual puppy requisites: bowls, two—one eating, one drinking; bed; collar and lead; brush, comb and toothbrush; realistic rubber toy that squeaks under pressure and some vitamin tablets for yourself, you will not have to put yourself out for the Virgoan's arrival into your home. He will adapt himself to whatever way of life you choose to lead, whether you get up at 5.30 a.m. or 10.30 a.m., have lunch instead of dinner or sleep with your window shut.

But he will want to have a say over some of the more material matters. He will take a great interest in the way you have arranged the furniture, the fabric you have chosen for the curtains and the pattern of the wallpaper. He will sift, sort and even try to re-arrange, until everything is how he likes it. Small chairs will be pushed towards their new position until you finally give in and leave them there; curtains, where he cannot reach the rails and feels that they could hang to better advantage in another room, will be pulled down and left in a heap; contents of cupboards will be moved laboriously to their proper place and even people will be made aware of the fact that the dog considers they are using the wrong room for the wrong function, and they will soon discover that to move will make life easier.

As with all the 'earthy' signs, this dog will have green-feet. He will take a genuine interest in your garden and spend a lot of his time increasing his knowledge of horticulture. He will weed—although he will not always be able to tell a seedling from a dandelion. He will dig, naturally, and try to keep the lawn under control by pulling up the grass. When visiting other peoples' gardens he will study their plants and methods in detail, taking cuttings of anything that he thinks would improve the garden at home. You will be wasting any time that you spend on trying to stop him wearing himself out on your behalf. Like all born gardeners, it was in him long before he set eyes on you and there will be nothing that can be done about it.

SOCIAL INTEGRATION

Virgo is a sign of service, and the Virgoan will never be happier than when he is doing something for you, taking over some of the little chores that pile up during the day. And he will have no further reward in mind beyond the knowledge that he has done his best to help someone less fortunate than himself.

He will rush down stairs to fetch the papers in the morning dribbling in his enthusiasm so that the front page disintegrates and you cannot read the headlines. He will take the dish-cloth to mop out his basket and drop it so that you never see it again. He will push books, sewing, glasses and pens underneath the sofa to save you the job of tidying the living room, and he will eat the remainder of Sunday's joint to save you the trouble of mincing it on Monday.

Then, in his spare time, he will perform more personal duties for you. He may decide that you really need a hot-water bottle that is not going to lose its heat during the coldest part of the night, and take the role upon himself. He will sit on your lap in the car when he sees that you can drive no farther without a rug to keep out the cold. He will hide your cigarettes because he knows that you are trying to give up smoking and he will bury your best hat because you so obviously suffer every time you wear it. And you will not be able to be cross with him. It will all have been done with the best intentions a dog could have—to make life easier for his owner.

The Virgoan will never be a forward dog. On the rare occasions when he does forget himself and issue an order his lack of practice will make it so obvious and give so much offence, that he will not try again for some time. His bossy, staccato barks will not encourage you to flatten yourself on the floor and reach for his ball with the poker because he has let it run to the back of the tallboy. Nor will ankle-biting make you rush out for a six mile hike, although you may put on your Wellingtons in self-defence.

Such lapses will be rare—unless there are children in the house. The Virgoan will definitely not be a family dog in the sense of baby-sitting or putting up with childish behaviour. Turning a blind eye to being used as a steam roller will b beyond him. He will never care for children, especially other peoples', finding them too unpredictable for his methodical mind.

But he will have one passion uncommon to dogs: he will adore cats. Fat cats, furry cats, bald cats and even kittens will give him more pleasure than spitting does to a camel. If you have a cat he will literally worship the ground it walks on, following it round the house and blowing at it lovingly. He will sit by it, wash it, want to take it to bed with him and have very little time left for anybody else. If the cat has had a traumatic experience with a dog and finds these advances frightening the Virgoan will be mystified but do his best to help. It has been known for a dog of this type to spend the night on the floor rather than disturb a cat that was frightened of him but had decided to use his bed for the night.

Your real trouble will come when the Virgoan meets strange cats, which will be unavoidable from time to time. To him cat will mean friend and whenever he sees one he will rush up and try to play with it. Cats who do not know him may well be frightened as he surges towards them in a frenzy of excitement. He will learn by experience that these ador- able creatures have needles in their feet, and become more cautious and less likely to come home with blood pouring off his nose.

The safest way of coming to an arrangement over this is to buy him a kitten. Expecting a family cat of long standing to take kindly to any dog, let alone one who is besotted with a blissful opinion of the use of cats, will be a bit too much. A kitten will not know any better if it grows up with the dog, it may even like him, and will not try to blind him every time he approaches.

All types of cat-loving people will find this dog pleasant and easy to have around the house, expect perhaps the Scorpionian who will see him as a tedious flatterer. Taureans will always

bring out the best in the Virgoan, and Capricornians will bring out the practical side of this dog in an unusually successful relationship.

PERSONAL RELATIONSHIPS

The Virgoan will not have much time for dogs, especially young ones. Apart from his affinity to cats he will be a lone-dog, impatient with the shortcomings so often found in animals of inferior intellect: the inability to purr, or tell you whether or not it will rain in the morning. He will avoid their company, unless he finds them chasing one of his friends when he will become really angry and quite vicious in his attack.

If you happen to own another dog, he will be most unhappy. He will want to keep himself to himself which will mean that you will have to have two gardens, two dog bedrooms, two dining rooms and probably two cars. Unless you want to be in a situation where you never know where one dog is because he has taken himself off to get some peace and quiet.

AMOROUS INCLINATIONS

If you bought a Virgoan in the hope of avoiding the problems that occur with some of the more randy types, you will have made a mistake. Only the very rare specimens will be happy without sex.

The average Virgoan will be nowhere near as loose as the Arian and his love affairs will be few and often unfortunate. But he will be discreet, preferring to keep such personal matters to himself. He will turn with disdain from obvious displays by other dogs, congratulating himself on knowing better than to behave in such a way himself.

Surprisingly enough the city of Paris is said to be heavily under the influence of Virgo.

PHYSICAL CHARACTERISTICS

The Virgoan will be strong and muscular, and if you want him to leave you alone at home the only thing to do will be to give him plenty of exercise. Physical fatigue will be practically unknown to this dog, unless you can work out a rota whereby members of the family divide twelve hours of the day into equal shifts so that there is always one of them taking him for a walk. Then he may sleep when he gets home, but he still may not. His wiry build will make him enjoy an endurance test of this kind, and he will have as much energy left as if it had just been a trip to the bus stop and back. He will turn into a tornado when you get back from a two hour walk, running through the house all down at the back, leaping from chair to chair and seeing how many times he can thump up and down the stairs before you hit him.

The Virgoan will deny that he is a healthy dog—which he will be for most of the time. He will be the hypochondriac to beat all others, turning the smallest patch of dandruff into bubonic plague and telling you that his tummy upset will not be cured by cod-liver oil because it is caused by his duodenal ulcer. Trips to the vet will be his one idea of a real outing, and once you have got him there you will have to drag him away by the scruff.

He will treat every meal that you place before him as a possible source of food poisoning and prefer his water to be freshly poured each time he feels thirsty than to be left stagnating to catch the falling dust. This fastidiousness will make him watch you prepare his dinner to see that you wash your hands before touching the meat, scour the bowl and then sterilize it and scrub the bit of floor you are going to put it on. If he has the slightest doubt about the way a meal has been served he will refuse to touch it for fear of bringing on an attack of his chronic acidosis.

JUST YOUR BAD LUCK

To find yourself with a primitive Virgoan will be unfortunate indeed. He will continually find fault with his circumstances, refusing to go into the garden because it is too small or complaining that you are expecting too much of him if it is too big. His bed will only be fit for a mongrel and he will bring up his meals.

Libra

September 24 to October 23

The sign of the Shop-Steward
A cardinal airy sign
Alert, just, painstaking, well balanced

Ruler: Venus

Harmonious signs: Aquarius, Gemini

Libra

BASIC TEMPERAMENT

The balance of Libra symbolises equality and justice and the Libran will be the trade unionist, the shop steward in dog's clothing who will devote his life to improving the conditions of the working or owned dog.

He will study his environment carefully, starting at the bottom and worming himself up to the top. This will take him a year or so, no longer, and then he will begin the ardous job of coming to terms with his owner. He will stand for less obedience for more food and a shorter working week. He will come out on strike for longer biscuit breaks and settle for no less than the practice of the closed shop—one house, one dog. He will not believe in work-sharing.

He will be genuinely frightened of all mechanical innovations seeing electrical grooming kits and clockwork toys as a direct threat to his position and the nearest things to the automated pet. He will expect a Christmas bonus and regular outings to keep his working morale up.

But he will be well balanced in himself, unlikely to suffer from unreasonable emotion, and he will be capable of considerable impartiality. He will be amiable and appreciative of the good things of life. Above all he will believe in share and share alike; measure for measure, or what is right for the owner is right for the dog and what is right for the dog is right for the owner.

LEBENSRAUM

There will be no banishing the Libran to a kennel at the bottom of the garden, unless you happen to prefer that way of life yourself. In fact it will be useless for anyone who believes in giving their dog a dog's life ever to consider having a Libran. This dog will only be suited to someone who intends to put themselves out for their dog, for no Libran will stand for being turned out into the cold while his owner stays inside beside the fire.

Providing you intend any dog of yours to lead as good a life as you do yourself, the Libran's attitude to living in a house will depend entirely on what you make of your circumstances. He will model his life pattern on yours so, if in the long run things go wrong, you will only have yourself to blame.

The Libran will know that what you do, he should do, and that wither goest thou, so must he. And he will keep himself so well informed as to what you are doing, that it will be impossible to fool him. You may try tucking yourself up on a safari bed in the kitchen each night but he will be well aware that no sooner have you heard his first snore than you creep up stairs and sink into the luxury of a deep feather bed. Humans sleep in beds, therefore so do dogs—and preferably the very same bed. He will creep up after you just as you are settling down with the pleasant thought that you have fooled him at last.

He will reason that if you have three meals a day one is not enough for him, and when you eat out of a bowl marked dog he will know intuitively that the contents are not stale biscuit and tinned meat.

He will soon learn that chairs are for sitting on and argue himself blue in the face if you try to keep him on the floor. He will also think that boots and a mackintosh are a very good idea when it is raining and cold.

On the other hand, he will be as generous as he is demanding, so ready to share his possessions with you that he will often make you feel how very mean you are. He will always move up to make room for you beside him on the sofa and when you give him a bone he will be deeply offended if you turn down his offer of a lick for a lick and a suck for a suck.

On the whole the Libran will be content with the little things of life, chasing mice in the garden, studying the aero-dynamics of a fly, picking up pins in his feet and eating dolly mixtures, so he will not take a lot of looking after. Although fairly easy where matters of eating, sleeping and exercise are concerned, there will be complications with this dog, and they will nearly always come from a totally unexpected quarter.

If you entertain a lot, asking friends to your house and offering them refreshment of one kind or another, the time will come when the Libran decides to follow your example once again. Your reaction on coming into the house and finding a dogs tea-party taking place in the living room will be a poor show compared to his when you turn all his friends out of the back door. You could try putting up a sign saying:

no traders, hawkers or other peoples' dogs. But the most successful cure will be to stop entertaining yourself.

However flattered you may feel you will never be able to forget that you are the example by which your dog lives: that he is watching your every move determined to emulate you. If he belches after meals and chews his cud between them it will be because you do.

The only time you will get in which to indulge yourself will be when the Libran is exhausted from the effort of keeping you under proper surveillance. His spurts of frantic energy will be followed by periods of sleep so deep that all his faculties will be resting and useless. Then, and only then, will you be able to have a good scratch, swear, pick your spots and generally wallow in impolite behaviour.

SOCIAL INTEGRATION

Despite his more infuriating characteristics the Libran will usually be as loved as he is loving, due to a remarkably gentle manner and a real desire to please. In a home where he is treated properly he will give out an air of contentment and well being that will touch everyone—one of the reasons that he will always get his own way more often than is good for him.

He will need affection and go out of his way to show his feeling for you in the hope that you will do the same to him, to give him the reassurance that he cannot do without.

But do not think for a moment that he will see only the good in you. To live like you he will have had to study you very closely and he will be as aware as you are that you are unsociable in the mornings, have a passion for the milkman and spend far too much of your time trying to find out what is going on next door. The fact that he very rarely brings any of these faults up when arguing with you, certainly not in public and only at

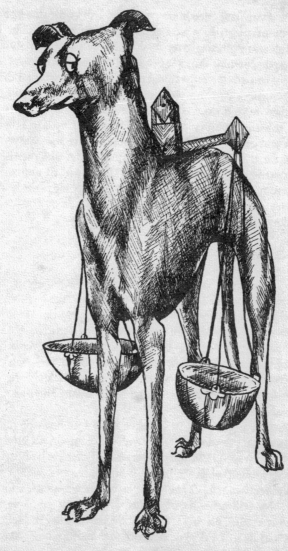

home if you have tried him very sorely, will be because he has a horror of upsetting you and turning you against him. His tactfulness in glossing over your bad points will be only able to be put down to this, not because he is blind to them.

Leonians are the most suited to surviving life with a Libran, the two signs reacting well and bringing out the best in one another rather than the worst. The Leonian supplies strength and constant reassurance which will bolster up the Libran's basic insecurity. Geminians and Aquarians are also compatible signs for the Libran, but Arians should never take the risk as their strong character will sap the Libran's small amount of self-confidence, so that he becomes an apology for a dog rather than a dog in his own right.

PERSONAL RELATIONSHIPS

The Libran will be as concerned over the living conditions of other dogs as he is his own. Worrying over the fact that the dog next door is not allowed to have any spare time to go off on its own will make him want to alter the situation. He will certainly interfere, either by helping the dog to make a hole in the fence or distracting it when it is meant to be playing ball with its owner, and your neighbours will quite rightly take the attitude that he is poking his nose into other peoples' affairs.

He will never learn that other dogs can be happy in a situation that he does not like and will continue to interfere even after he has been warned off, so that there will always be trouble around when the Libran is out with other dogs. It will be indirect trouble, for the Libran will never attack another dog, that will arise out of his inability to let well alone and his insistence on playing the role of the peacemaker and referee.

When he sees a dog with a stick and another dog standing

by longingly, he will see fit to remove the stick and hand it to the other dog. It is the latter who will be attacked for stealing when the deprived dog comes to, the Libran by that time having no connection with the offending article.

At other times he will try to pour oil on troubled waters quickly summing up the cause of a dog fight. If the fight is over a bitch, he will remove her, so that the two dogs sign a truce and join forces to attack him. If two dogs are fighting simply for the fun of it the Libran will set up a diversion—a cat chase or rabbit hunt—until the fight is stopped. The result of this pacifist behaviour will be one bewildered Libran, bitten and bruised, and mystified as to the reason. He will never learn to leave other dogs to their own affairs and will continue to place himself in danger throughout his life.

AMOROUS INCLINATIONS

The airy Libran will spend a lot of his time getting involved with the opposite sex, but it will always be in the most tactful way. He will know instinctively that to show his feelings for a bitch is not the thing to do, unless his owner makes a practice of it, and he will behave with planned disinterest until he has lured her behind the garage or into the woods.

Dog owners will always think what a nice civilised dog the Libran is and never connect him with any misfortunes that may befall their pets. Which will make life easy for you as you will not lose any friends through his behaviour.

The female Libran will also be tactful, but in a different sort of way. She will be so afraid of offending any dog that she will find it impossible to say 'no'. This misguided consideration will mean that she will always have to be sent away in a delicate condition, or locked in a dungeon, or strapped in a chastity belt.

On top of this she will be the worst mother imaginable, disowning her offspring from the moment they enter the world. This lack of maternal instinct will mean that you will have to feed the puppies from their first day. Regular snacks with a pen-filler will be as necessary at night as they are during the day. While the mother is off on the tiles again you will be teaching eight little mouths how to lap, cleaning up after them and giving them the security they should be having from her.

Unfortunately neither sex will improve with age. The female Libran will never connect having puppies with anything she has done so she will not make any attempts to avoid what is obviously distasteful to her. The male will be the prototype dirty old dog. When he is on his death bed he will still be worrying about adding more heirs to his never-ending family tree, and it will surprise you what reserves of energy he will have to draw upon when under the urge. An old dog that has to be carried upstairs and wheeled out in a bath-chair will think nothing of running up and down a one-in-nine hill three times a day when his lady-love lives at the top.

Tranquillisers from the vet may help, or hormone injections, but as long as your dog is happy you should not worry too much.

PHYSICAL CHARACTERISTICS

The slogan 'fair, fat and forty' is commonly believed to have been originally stated about a middle aged Libran woman. In fact it was inspired by an elderly Libran bitch, and is true of all dogs of this type. Throughout their life they will appear well-nourished, as indeed they will always see that they are, but as they grow older these earlier indulgences will catch up with them so that they begin to bulge and spread around the waist.

Whatever his age, when the Libran shows signs of not being quite himself with a dry nose and no enthusiasm for anything, the best cure will be a diet. You will never go wrong with this, although he will not like it at the time. His recovery will often be instantaneous with his first calory-counted meal, but you should carry it on for a period of convalescence. Every ounce saved when he is young will mean an inch less when he is older, a fact he would be bound to appreciate if you could only make him understand.

JUST YOUR BAD LUCK

The primitive Libran will be a dabbler, having so many interests and friends that his owner will never know where he is or what he is up too. His portrayal of the original copy-dog will be so accurate that there will be nothing at all you can do without him doing it too. It has been known for this type to insist on bathing with his owner on top of everything else, despite a dislike for water and a very small bath.

Because of his total belief in equality he will lose himself in his efforts to share his owner's life and reach the stage of being unable to make up his mind for himself over the simplest matters.

He will also believe that every second member of the opposite sex is the one for him and in his enthusiasm will forgo the respectability of the more evolved type. Innocence will be his worst enemy, and if you have picked one of these dogs, the best, indeed the only way, will be to teach him as much as possible, by example.

Scorpio

October 24 to November 22

The sign of the Governor or Paragon
A fixed watery sign
Energetic, independent, determined, with strong likes and dislikes

Ruler: Mars

Harmonious signs: Cancer, Pisces, Scorpio

Scorpio

BASIC TEMPERAMENT

SCORPIO is a fixed and watery sign symbolising power . . . and the ability to sting. The dog born under it will have great strength of character concealed beneath his silky coat and, if without an actual sting built into his tail, will be well able to achieve a similar effect with that part of his anatomy when the occasion demands it.

He will be a formidable dog to live up to, for if it is possible for any dog to be perfect, this would be the one. His life will be spent pursuing but one ambition: complete self-mastery. Succumbing to the weaknesses of nature will not be his idea of how a dog should conduct himself and he will go to great lengths to creat practical situations that will stretch his powers of endurance.

He will bravely break a milk bottle, overcoming his fear of getting glass in his feet, by knocking it off the step before you have noticed that the milkman has been. Then he will force himself to watch the contents until the last drop has seeped into the ground. It will be nothing to him to sit so closely to a plate of chocolate cakes that water drools from his mouth and falls in a sticky puddle by his feet. Each time he fails this test he will start again, only giving in when there is nothing left on the plate to tempt him.

He will go on trying throughout his life, happily unaware that the perfect state he seeks will never be within his capabilities. He will be let down—even in old age—by a mind that will be as difficult for him to understand as it will for his owners.

LEBENSRAUM

With the Scorpionian you are going to have that which all other dog owners claim to despise and usually have themselves: a dog-owned house. The Scorpionian will treat your house as a kingdom in which he is the only person who carries any weight and he will expect you to respect this situation by running it for him to his specifications. If you fail to realise this he will train you, pointing out your mistakes and only making much of you when you behave correctly.

If he happens to use the living room for his bedroom because it is the warmest room in the house with the most comfortable bed, you will be expected to leave him alone in it early enough for him to have the full eight hours of undisturbed sleep which is so necessary to a dog's well-being. Should you be rash enough to sit up for the Late Show or the Midnight Movie he will tell you that your time is up, by snoring and fidgeting and sighing very heavily. He will be very obviously 'being kept awake' and will be of the opinion that if you really must stay up the least you could do would be to turn the sound off.

His firm belief that nature can be improved upon will not

be confined to the house. A Scorpionian on holiday at the seaside has been known to spend hours daring the incoming waves to income a step farther; he was as unsuccessful as Canute. He will go frantic in the rain, order it not to land in his garden and when it refuses to obey him, loose his temper on an unsuspecting stick which will be worried to death.

Nearly all Scorpionians will be psychic to some extent and despite their efforts to remain inscrutable in times of stress, will make it only too clear when they are 'seeing' something. When you are sitting peacefully of an evening trying to forget that you are alone in the house and the wind is whistling in the trees outside, the Scorpionian will leap to his feet, his hackles bristling along his spine, and bark despairingly at an empty corner of the room. When he has made you thoroughly frightened, he will relax as if nothing untoward has happened. It will be safe for you to turn round then, for it will mean that the visitor has left through the wall he used to come in by.

The fact that the Scorpionian can hear a lot of things that other people cannot will be worth remembering if you have to spend a lot of the time alone in a house with one. If he starts to listen intently, putting his head first on one side and then on the other, it will not necessarily mean that a man with a revolver is creeping round the side of the house trying to find a way in. It will be far more likely some long dead relation calling him up on a wavelength that is beyond a mere human's powers of reception. Only when he is so frightened that you cannot get him out from under the bed will it be time to call the police for help.

SOCIAL INTEGRATION

Another Scorpionian is the ideal person to have a Scorpionian dog. They will have the same urge for power which will result in clashes of personality but they will have a full understanding for each other's position, so the quarrels will be more of a stimulant than anything else. A house with one Scorpionian in it—let alone two—could never be described as a haven of peace. It will be far more like a battleground with the commanders of the opposing sides fighting out of pure enjoyment.

The next person, indeed the only other person to stand a chance against the Scorpionian, will be the Cancerian. Some people say that Pisces can stand the strain, but they should only put it to the test as a last resort. Everyone else should avoid this type, for getting along with humans will not come naturally to him.

The Scorpionians ambition for control will not only cover himself. He will see it as far-reaching, to take in all those around him as well. The people who live with him will be expected to do as he tells them—promptly and without fuss.

You will have to teach him the hard way that you do not like a dog that is bossy and hard to please. When he demands attention or orders you to fetch this and that, not forgetting the other on the way, you will have to disobey him, flagrantly. You will have to ignore his tantrums, flount his demands and never give in to him once. And the Scorpionian will thrive on strict treatment. For nothing will ever be more congenial to him than the effort of breaking down the opposition in a battle of wits.

As long as you never forget that you are bigger than he is—a fact he will try to disprove by spending a lot of his time on table tops and looking down at you from half way up the stairs—and that you have more brain, you should be able to put him where you want him and keep him there, even if it means using a padlock.

Quarrelling aside, the Scorpionian will be an affectionate dog beneath his prickly exterior. But he will rarely show that he likes you, being far more reticent over this side of his nature

than when he is disapproving. He will shy away from sentimentality, bite anyone who tries to pet him, and never lower himself to the extent of being caught sitting on your lap.

PERSONAL RELATIONSHIPS

The Scorpionian will see other dogs as so dull as to be hardly worthy of his attention. When a strange dog takes a stand and challenges his superiority the Scorpionian will not hesitate to put him in his proper place. His anger will be sudden and extreme; the Scorpionian will not be able to limit his feelings in a proper relation to the cause, and many a bedraggled dog has gone home sadder and wiser, never to overstep the mark by saying 'good morning' to this type of dog again.

AMOROUS INCLINATIONS

In love Scorpionians will tend to be intense and exclusive. They will also suffer from a form of insecurity that will make it difficult for them to show their feelings. Only when they are deeply moved will they lose this reserve, to become far more forthcoming than the occasion demands. Once again, the animal side they try so hard to control, will have run away with them and let them down.

The Scorpionian bitch will be as intensely interested in sex as the male, and she will refuse to accept any limitations that should be imposed because of her sex. When locked up she will find a way out, for she will have a natural scorn for the female dog that shirks motherhood and will be completely at a loss as how to employ her energies if denied these possibilities herself.

Spaying will not help, except to frustrate her further. Some people do say that the best way to manage this type is to let her have puppies at the earliest opportunity to get it out of her system. Others say that this will only make her suffer from the twice yearly phantom pregnancy, which can be more trouble than the actual puppies. The answer will have to be decided by you, and your dog.

PHYSICAL CHARACTERISTICS

The thick-set Scorpionian will pride himself on his command of his handsome features. He will practice at resisting giving himself away however deeply he may be moved until he has achieved complete immobility of expression. When you threaten to punish him he will be as unmoved as he was when you came home from a three week holiday; sitting calmly as if nothing more terrible was happening than a fly walking upside down on the ceiling.

Unfortunately this is another dog that will be prone to middle-age spread. Unless you take stringent control over his food consumption all the time he is still growing. His naturally heavy build will look good for a few years and then suddenly, almost as he passes the half-way line of life, it will seem gross and unattractive.

Apart from this, which after all can easily be taken care of, the Scorpionian will be extraordinarily healthy, delighting in showing off his powers of endurance as yet another sign that mind can succeed over matter if you have the build for it. He will often defy the laws of health purely for the fun of it by spending a day lying in the rain and then refusing to let you towel him down so that he has to go to bed wet. At other times he will take himself off for days covering a considerable distance to prove that he can fend for himself and do without rest even when he is exhausted. He will not mind that you have to account for chickens stolen while he was away. And when the police ring you to please come and collect your dog because it is eating all their biscuits some thirty miles away, you will look at the bus time tables to see if he could have done it that way. But he won't have done. He will have actually walked—or run—until he could go no farther, and having proved his point will not want to have the effort of getting himself home again.

When ill, the Scorpionian will be really ill. A poor miserable dog with listless eyes and a nose that you could cook the dinner on will collapse in a heap in a very obvious place until you do something about it. A rest cure would be the best remedy, if you could ever persuade the dog. He will not be a good patient and will fret peevishly if life becomes too boring. He will grumble and complain at everything you try to do for him, blow out any pills he is meant to take and spill his medicine all over his bed.

Professional nursing will be the best way of ensuring a complete recovery without complications setting in so send him straight to kennels where they will not put up with any nonsense.

This dog will be inclined to have bow legs unless care is taken to give him enough bone-building vitamins when he is a puppy.

JUST YOUR BAD LUCK

The primitive Scorpionian will be an extreme example of his more normal—in comparison—counterpart. He will be thoroughly bad, quick to take offence, incessantly jealous and ridiculously over-impressed by his inflated ego.

He will not be capable of the smallest degree of sensitivity and will revel in finding the weak spots in those around him.

Then, when he has found them, he will work on them until the person on whom he is fixing his unpleasant attention can stand it no longer and hits out at him.

His sense of humour will be limited to the childish type of tripping people up, dropping bones into their food and slipping dead rats down their beds on clean-sheet day.

Sagittarius

November 23 to December 21

The sign of the Problem-dog or Muddler
A mutable fiery sign
Candid, restless, impulsive, impatient

Ruler: Jupiter

Harmonious signs: Aries, Leo, Sagittarius

Sagittarius

BASIC TEMPERAMENT

THIS will be a problem dog, a dog with a problem all his own that no one can help him with: to which of the two forces at play within him does he truly belong—the canine or the equine?

At times he will not know whether to wag his tail or use it to keep the flies out of his eyes; whether to bite the postman or nuzzle his pockets for sugar.

There will be whole days when he is definitely a dog and follows a pattern of behaviour that is easily recognisable to that form of life. He will get up only when he finds it impossible to stay indoors a minute longer. He will play with a bone or two, chase a couple of cats, worry you until you take him for a walk, bolt his supper and go contentedly to sleep in front of the fire.

Then there will be the bad days when he will graze on the lawn until he has made himself sick, or imagine that he is too big to squeeze through the back door yet big enough to jump the garden gate and take himself for a gallop in the woods. He will refuse to eat meat, demanding a bran-mash instead, and expect to be rugged up before you muck him out for the night.

The pressure from each in turn will be so strong that no sooner has he decided that he is really a dog, than he will start to neigh in his sleep. He will never be able to make a final decision to follow one trait and abandon the other so that his life will be spent in the continual conflict that arises out of divided loyalties.

LEBENSRAUM

You will learn to watch for the warning signs when he wakes each morning so that you will know well in advance whether you are the owner of a dog or a horse that day. If he takes off with your dressing-gown cord and buries it among the sofa cushions you will be safe in assuming that all is well, but if he is asleep standing up and looks for his breakfast in the bucket you should either hobble him, or tether him on the lawn for the day. Unless, of course, you have a stable to shut him in where he will be perfectly happy with a hay-net and a salt-block.

On the rare occasions when he is not absorbed with the heavy responsibilities arising from his peculiarity he will concentrate his powers of mental activity on the high ambition of getting to the bottom of it all, or reducing things to their simplest form. Carpets will revert to piles of nylon-mix and stranded wool, cardboard boxes to pulp. He will unearth the roots of rose trees and inspect the foundations of your house; empty dustbins, chocolate boxes and waste-paper baskets and search for hidden treasure in your shopping bag.

The Sagittarian will be a great believer in the out-of-doors life. To him flats and houses will be unhealthy stuffy places, and if inflicted upon him unnecessarily, they will be doomed from the start. Like the archer he will know instinctively where to aim to cause the most discomfort to others with the least effort to himself. He will know that stockings ladder; that you are frightened of mice whether they be dead or alive; that you will not go to bed without your curlers, and that shoes cannot be worn without laces.

If you are houseproud he will delight in turning out a room for you by pulling down the cushions, emptying the ashtrays onto the carpet, dusting the ornaments with his tail and removing dead flowers from their vases. It will be nothing to him to strip down a bed and throw slippers and night clothes out of the window. If you suffer from headaches he will make his point with the piercing bark so typical of the Sagittarian, that can penetrate several thicknesses of wall without losing its individual quality of tone.

A large garden which he can enjoy from first light until you are too tired to wait up for him any longer will ease the pressure on your nerves. Then he will be able to savour the morning air and satisfy his interest in nature by joining in the dawn chorus. He will occupy himself with geological research despite your constant warnings that stones are bad for his teeth and not to leave them lying about because of the lawn mower, and then put in some extra practice on his other favourite hobby, difficult exploration.

As the Sagittarian finds it impossible to learn from anybody but himself, he will do so only by first hand experience and slowly at that. He will repeat each investigation over and over again, falling into the same mistakes each time. The Jack

Russell born under this sign will continue to get lost and stuck down rabbit holes until he has covered every one within a five mile radius of your home. You will develop a phobia about endless nights spent digging by torch light. You will tell him each time you get him out that he is not to do it again. But he will see your rescue bids as a sign of your genuine interest in his activities, a sign of which all Sagittarians are very appreciative, and will continue to provide you with the opportunities for indulging yourself.

SOCIAL INTEGRATION

The Sagittarian will be an independent dog who will want to choose his friends for himself. The fact that you paid out a small fortune at an exclusive kennels will not carry any more weight with him than if you had rescued him from the local pound for seven and sixpence. He will either like you or dislike you purely on your merits as a person.

If he does not find you congenial you will be treated like any other of his casual acquaintances, only he will have to spend more time with you because you both happen to live in the same house. He will be polite nearly all the time, aloof and uninterested as long as he gets regular meals and a roof over his head at night. Most of the time he will be out visiting the friends that he has chosen.

However, should he find that the two of you have points in common he will be loyal and affectionate but still detached; at least compared to other dogs, as he will refuse to become completely wrapped up in any one person. He will still have other friends with whom he will want to associate.

The most successful way of bringing up the young Sagittarian will be to try to keep things down to his level. Furnish a room with half-size furniture, sleep on the floor and move

around the house on your hands and knees. Explain to him by imitating the action exactly what it is that you are trying to teach him. Sit when you say 'sit', lie when you say 'lie' and stop biting your feet when you say 'no'. You may find he gets amusement from this and sticks his nose in your face when you are sitting on the floor and lies on top of you when you are lying down but he will be ready enough to learn once you have made him understand the reason for your request. For instance—if you can explain to him that walking to heel will stop him from choking on his lead.

But he will test your reason, and you will wish you had never bothered if he finds out that walking to heel means getting kicked in the teeth by the back-end of your boot. The fact that he will learn only by his own experience will make him query almost anything you teach him, and the way he goes about this will be most ingenious.

If you have taught him that your dog does not accompany you to church he will want to know why. He will leave the house before you so that you cannot lock him in, and then appear in the middle of the aisle having sneaked through the door with one of the late entrants. If he finds it boring he will not bother again. But if he decides to put to the test the rule that your dog does not sit around on the furniture you will have to resort to putting boards across the seats of easy-chairs and hairbrushes under the covers, until he really does believe that they are as uncomfortable as you said they were.

This dog's favourite person will be the Arian, in any shape or size. His zest for adventure will give the Sagittarian plenty to think about, and the two bring out only the best in one another. The Leonian will also get on very well with the Sagittarian while two Sagittarians will be the next best thing. Any other type will do better to try another kind of dog.

PERSONAL RELATIONSHIPS

The Sagittarian will come into contact with other dogs as easily as he does humans—unobtrusively, meeting them when he is out on his own or out of sight behind a tree. He will have no time for dogs that he does not feel a personal affinity for and his skill in dialectic will make him merciless with any foolish suggestions. And once his hackles are up he will be a formidable fighter.

The archer in him will know exactly where to strike; the ears, eyes and tail of the other dog, or any sensitive spot like a bad leg or half-healed battle wound. He will also know where the arteries are closest to the surface, and very seldom miss his mark. If you are out with him and see trouble coming you will do well to publicly disown him on the spot and punish him severely when you have reached the privacy of your own home.

AMOROUS INCLINATIONS

This dog will need a lot of sympathy during times of love because he will invariably fall for a dog that cannot return his feelings. She will either be firmly behind glass in the local pet-shop window or kept under lock and key by unfortunate owners. The Sagittarian will suffer deeply from the pangs of unrequited love, going right off his food and refusing to find any enjoyment in life.

Age may teach him that there is more fun for a dog in not falling for the untouchable. Then he will shun the dogs with breeding, preferring those whom nobody would bother to lock up anyway.

The female Sagittarian will be as frustrated as the male, but for a different reason. Her frank, blunt attitude to sex will be fully appreciated by other dogs, which will not have been what she meant at all. She will take offence at their precociousness unaware that it was her fault in the first place. The male dog will retire, wiser, and not bother with her any more, which again will not have been what she meant. She may learn in the end, but she is more likely to go through life never getting further than a mild flirtation. She will not be a dog you could count on for breeding.

PHYSICAL CHARACTERISTICS

Vitality oozes out of the Sagittarian at every paw. He will have the well-balanced body that lends itself to taking energetic exercise; his eyes will be bright and shining, his nose wet and healthy, his feet and ankles will be fine and delicate. Unless he happens to be too heavily influenced by the equine force, when his body will be of unusual shape for a dog, his feet high and with very small toes, his nose too big, his ears too pointed and his neck too long.

Whichever type he is, he will express his feelings with vigorous unexpected gestures that could never be described as graceful. When you come home from an outing he will either jump right into your basket or bruise your legs with his tail. When he wants something he will run around and thump his tail so loudly on the carpet that dust you have not seen for years will come rushing to the surface. When he is comfortable he will snore—and snore.

He will be healthier than most, only coming to harm when he is too active. It will be aches, sprains, pains and bruises that make you send for the vet, all of which the Sagittarian will suffer before declining years make him settle down and take things easy.

The one thing you will have to watch for will be hiccups.

He will know that if a horse once gets an attack there is no stopping it and it hiccups to an untimely death. If it happens to be one of those days, the Sagittarian will truly believe that this is what is happening to him, and once he has got that idea there will be very little that anyone can do about it, beyond giving him the fright of his life.

JUST YOUR BAD LUCK

The primitive Sagittarian will be an *enfant terrible* when he is young, a juvenile delinquent later and end up as a thimble-rigger first class. However, astrologers have long said that the Sagittarians faults are 'those that are easily pardoned', which may make you feel better when you find yourself constantly doing just that.

This dog will never be vicious—his one redeeming point— as he will be free from the complex emotions that bring this about nor will he steal or bite people.

Capricorn

December 22 to January 20

The sign of the Snob or Social Climber
A cardinal earthy sign
Ambitious, persevering, diplomatic, reserved

Ruler: Saturn

Harmonious signs: Taurus, Virgo, Libra

Capricorn

BASIC TEMPERAMENT

THE goat symbolises ambition and an ability to scale heights that will be the driving force behind all dogs born under Capricorn, for this is the sign of the snob, or social climber.

This dog will have an interest in class and social standing that will verge on the indecent, being able to sum up in one glance just what sort of a person you are, whether you were brought up or dragged up, born in a palace or a slum. No amount of pretending on your part in the way of voice training or deportment will fool him, he will see through it all and think no more of you for your trouble.

The Capricornian's determination to better his position in the world will preoccupy him to the exclusion of everything else. And he will be willing to accept from you anything that will help him to this end; training; sessions at the beauty parlour and even advanced obedience tests. Being naturally reserved and diplomatic, he will be a most amenable dog knowing that the nicer he appears to others the more likely he is to succeed in life.

He will also have a keen interest in the past which, when he is not working out your personal history or name dropping, will involve him in archaeological research. Remains, however high, will be studied thoroughly and subjected to searching tests such as those necessary to discover the lasting properties of the scent when carefully placed behind the ears. ·

His owner will rest assured in the knowledge that nothing the Capricornian does is without reason. He will have rolled in the smell because this is the only sure way he knows of getting a bath out of you, and he wants to look his best for Lady So-and-So who is coming to tea tomorrow.

The ladder of life will be a very real thing to the Capricornian and as surely as rockets fly to the moon, he will work his way up it rung by rung, with you not far behind him.

LEBENSRAUM

Ideally the Capricornian would like to be in the position of the Royal Corgis, right at the top of his profession. Finding himself in an average household he will be smart enough to know that the bigger the success he makes of it the more likely his puppies will be to better themselves.

He will adapt to his environment easily. The bigger and more ostentatious your home, the more he will approve of you, but to start with poor conditions will not worry him unduly, they will merely put him on his mettle to carry you up with him.

As he becomes older and more aware of the ways of the world he will nudge you gently up the social scale. He will get very cross if you inisist on dunking your biscuits when you are out, barking frantically in the hope of creating a diversion to give you time to remember yourself while eyes are turned in his direction. Should you try to go to the shops with your hair in curlers, he will refuse to go with you making no secret of his disapproval. Should you be going out to Bingo or Ten-pin bowling, he will make such a mess of the house that you will never go and leave him alone again. On the

other hand, if you are going to night-school with a view to improving your prospects you will find no dog more pleased to be left by himself.

This dog will attach great importance to anything connected with a higher way of life. He will be well aware that top people believe hunting, shooting and fishing should automatically be among the accomplishments of civilised beings, and he will put in a lot of time improving his standard in these sports. Beagling will be his favourite of the three, and singleminded as he is, you will find it impossible to call him off once he is on the scent. He will be deaf to the world, and no amount of screaming will bring him back. You may notice how often this will happen towards the end of a walk. Whether he bribes the hares you will never know. But they will always be going in the opposite direction to your home, putting at least half an hour onto the twenty minutes you had allowed for dog walking that day.

SOCIAL INTEGRATION

This will be the Capricornian's forte. Unlike other dogs he will admit that the will of the majority should have control if life is to be smooth and untroubled. And as in his circle the will of the majority will be human, he will be obedient, generally accepting rules and regulations.

He will admit the necessity for restraint, and never run away when you want to put on his lead. It will not be beyond the very sensitive Capricornian to put his head in the loop to save you trouble. But do not think this is through any lack of self-esteem. It will be because he knows that if he does not accept the lead he will be left behind, and then how would he get out and about to meet the right people?

The Capricornian's ability to tell at a glance the social standing of everyone who comes to your house could well be disconcerting. He will pay far more attention to the vicar than he does to the man who comes to read the meter, and postmen and burglars will be completely ignored. On the other hand should you have any friends among the peerage dropping in for a chat, he will become positively fawning.

Two Capricornians social climbing together will have a splendid relationship, but the most suitable owner for this dog will be the blue-blooded Virgoan, down to earth enough to keep the Capricornian from becoming too obsessed with his standing in life and also likely enough to be a success himself and so able to offer the Capricornian the things he needs. Taureans and Librans will also find this dog compatible, but Sagittarians should leave well alone.

PERSONAL RELATIONSHIPS

This dog will be a dog after any serious breeder's heart being as aware as he is of the necessity of pedigrees and pure strains. The perfect stud dog that you could use to found a line of budding champions because he will turn away from a poor specimen, however tempting she may be.

With an instinct that could well be used by the compilers of the Kennel Club files, he will head immediately for the most acceptable dog of a group. He will cultivate the better class of dog as he does humans, spurning all mongrels as if they were vermin. With a dog of the right standing he will be so obsequious in his preliminaries that they will become the best of friends. Should a lesser breed try to pass the time of day with him he will be freezingly disapproving. The liberty taker will be seen off sharply, cut to the quick by the Capricornian's disdain, as he does not even bother to follow once the offender has turned tail, passing off the whole thing as a complete misfortune. Really, what is the world coming to?

AMOROUS INCLINATIONS

The Capricornian will be so sex concious and frustrated by his own snobbishness that when faced with a bitch of suitable class he will be unable to control himself at all, getting over-excited and most embarrasing. This state of affairs will arise out of the most innocent situation where there is no possible cause for alarm and the female has not given him any encouragement at all.

This constant urge to challenge the opposite sex will be the one and only time when the Capricornian will forget himself and behave in a way that will do nothing to help him on in life. The results will not always be of the most desirable type. Outraged dog owners—and even outraged dogs—will not invite him to their homes again; they may even drop you as well. So to save your dog, and yourself, from social disappointment you will be wise to check on the sex and breeding of dogs in the houses you are likely to visit.

The female Capricornian will waken to the joys of motherhood late in life. Feeding and weaning will be a bore to her and the more help you can give her the more chance of survival the puppies will have. But when it comes to the time to find homes for her offspring, they will receive her undivided attention.

Potential puppy buyers will be submitted to an extensive scrutiny, and should they not come up to her standards they will not be allowed near the brood. She will stand guard, growling and warding off any attempts to approach her hitherto neglected litter by casting any aspersions she can bring to mind. Should they prove acceptable, she will throw the puppy at them without a second thought.

PHYSICAL CHARACTERISTICS

Many of the world's most beautiful dogs have been born under this sign, and without exception all Capricornians will approach perfection in form and build. This is probably because of the infinite care they themselves take when breeding. Any weakness that will show will be an over-long nose and underslung jaw, which they are doing their best to breed out.

Instead of losing his looks early in life the Capricornian will tend to mature late and continue to look his best long after other dogs are on the decline. And providing they are in congenial surroundings they stand a good chance of a longer life span than is normally found in dogs.

You may run into health problems with this type if, by the time he reaches middle age, you show no further sign of improving your position in life. Deep depression will set in and he will give up the fruitless task of showing you the way, taking a defeatist attitude to life. If this situation does arise and the dog no longer cares whether you go outside in your slippers and eat your peas off your knife, the only thing you will be able to do to stop him pining away completely will be to pull yourself together and remember that he is your dog and deserves what he wants.

If this is impossible, you could give him to someone with the required status so that he can enjoy his final years in peace of mind.

JUST YOUR BAD LUCK

The primitive Capricornian will start life weighed down by the impossibility of it all. He will be a despondent puppy, and a deadly dull adult. He will realise that you have bought him and he has to stay with you, and if you do not live in a pent house in Park Lane his life will be doomed before it has begun.

His frustrated ambition will consume him, until he becomes a shadow of an animal who skulks around the house and is ashamed to show his face outside it. He will feel that other dogs are laughing at him, and blame it all on you. He will be so obsessed with his own meagre interests that he will withdraw into himself and forget to be pleasant to other people refusing to make any allowances for their faults and lack of ambition.

He will only cheer up on the rare occasions when you use the silver tea-service or hire staff for a dinner party. Then he will rally round only until the last butler leaves the house and the sugar bowl is once again locked up, when he will sink back into his shell and dream of days gone by when things were not so bad.

Aquarius

January 21 to February 19

The sign of the Truth-seeker or Pacifist
A fixed airy sign
Honest, probing, amiable, humane, popular

Ruler: Uranus

Harmonious signs: Libra, Gemini, Aries

Aquarius

BASIC TEMPERAMENT

AQUARIUS is another of the 'fixed' signs and the dog born under it will be determined in a quiet, inoffensive way, to find the truth about everything and everyone he comes across. The Aquarian will be the truth-seeker of dogs to whom knowing a little is tantamount to knowing nothing at all.

When he gets a fix on the scent of a quarry the fact that the animal in question is obviously a rabbit—or hare, or woozle—will not be enough. He will want to know which rabbit;

why it was in such a hurry; how many brothers and sisters it has; whether it lost a lot of relations in the great epidemic and how long it has been living in the district. To get this information he will have to go right back to the beginning, so instead of following the rabbit he will take the scent in the opposite direction. A point that makes these dogs unsuited for the working life of hunting dogs, but very popular with members of the League Against Blood-sports.

He will be neither militant nor aggressive in his painstaking search for the truth, just aggravatingly slow if you are trying to get somewhere on time. Like the Mafia, he will be able to wait. When he finds a smell beside the road he will study it until he could tell you—if it was possible—not only what the depositor of the smell had for dinner the night before but his name and address as well.

There will be times when his persistence works to your advantage instead of getting in the way. If a burglar was rude enough to climb in through the window the Aquarian would not consider him a friend simply because he had one bone in his pocket. But if the burglar is familiar with the workings of the Aquarian mind and has several bones in each pocket and dog-chocolates in his turn-ups, you will go downstairs in the morning to find that you not only have to contact the police, but also the vet to bring out an antidote for tummy ache.

LEBENSRAUM

The Aquarian will be very little trouble about the house. He will not be unnecessarily noisy, nor will he rush about creating havoc like some of the more airy types. He will be quiet—so quiet—that as you dash from room to room to see what he has been up to in the three hours since you last heard him you will be right to fear what you are going to find.

This dog will never be happier than when he can devote a whole morning to undisturbed study. He may want to increase his knowledge about the inside workings of a camera, or find out if every pack of cards had two jokers, four aces, twelve picture cards and an odd assortment covered with different coloured dots.

You will have to watch him to avoid too much damage to your possessions. A stock of elementary 'teaching' toys as used in infants' classes will help, while you might manage to get him interested in the car maintenance lectures on television. Only, if you do, be careful to lock the garage and hang the keys on a hook in the ceiling.

SOCIAL INTEGRATION

Aquarius is the eleventh sign of the Zodiac, closely linked with the eleventh house of the horoscope, which tells of a dog's relationship with humanity—the most important aspect of the Aquarian.

Your dog will be friendly not only to you but the whole of the human race, up to a point and no further until he has weighed a person up. A visitor will be followed round the house while the dog picks up all the information that can be gleaned from footprints, backs of legs and the bottom of clothes. Then the visitor will be sat by, but the look on the dog's face will not be the one of adoration that the visitor claims it to be—"Animals always like me, they know, you know". It will be a look of scrutiny and will be wiped off as soon as the dog has decided that the person is all right, if uninteresting.

Geminians and Librans will be the most likely people to pass this examination of their personal habits and be chosen as friends by the Aquarian. And of the two, the Libran will have a head start because he will have the same intelligent preference for working things out rather than jumping to conclusions that is found in the Aquarian. At times they will have differences of opinion—which they will both enjoy—but they will always remain a little independent from each other which will save them from becoming so involved that they come to blows.

The Geminian and the Aquarian will develop almost as successful a relationship, but the former's stubborn streak will cause occasional friction. After a while the Aquarian will learn how to avoid this side of the Geminian, so that when he does want his own way he will get it without too much fuss.

Providing you are not an Arian, the one person who will invariably bring out the worst in the Aquarian, this dog will be affectionate and surprisingly eager to learn. So much so, that at times you will be driven to question his motives. Does he come running every time you call him because he genuinely wants to do as you want him to, or is it because he knows about the biscuit you have hidden in your hand?

More often than not it will be for another reason: one that only the dog is aware of. He may be measuring up the room in which you are holding the training session, or he may be finding out how quickly a dog can reach maximum speed from a sitting start. But whatever the reason, providing he is doing what you wish, there will be nothing to worry about.

When you tell him that it is more civilised for a dog to spend his pennies in the garden rather than in the house his eagerness to remember will not be through any understanding of your dislike of mopping up after him. He will be comparing the absorbent qualities of carpet and crazy-paving, newspaper to grass and rush matting to flower-beds.

Through his need to find everything out for himself he will attach very little importance to tradition or authority. When faced with them he will be polite, and may be slightly

interested, but he will not go beyond the natural call of good manners if he does not want to.

At times his thoroughness and determination to take nothing at face value will be exceedingly tedious for you. He will never be beside himself with delight at a new toy you have bought him, or a strip of chewing gum that you thought might make up for the quarrel you had in the morning when he worked out how to open—and empty—the refrigerator. Anything like this will be taken from your hand as gingerly as possible and quickly pushed into a dark corner in case it is going to blow up. When he has watched it from a safe distance and assured himself on this point, he may push it gently, sniff at it and even move it to a more open position. Only when he is fully satisfied that it has no hidden detonators and is completely safe, which may take him a day or a week from the time that you gave it to him, will he suddenly be overcome by the sheer delight of possessing such an object. Then he will do all the things that a more satisfying dog would have done in the first place, like barking at it, throwing it over his shoulder and squashing it to death.

Unfortunately loyalty is not a quality found in Aquarians. This dog will have a bad memory, forgetting a person in the short space of time that another dog would take to tree a cat. If you do find yourself faced with the problem of what to do with your dog while you go away for two years, give him to friends. If you lend him to your neighbours he will not remember you when you come to claim him and not only will you lose your dog, but some friends as well.

PERSONAL RELATIONSHIPS

To the Aquarian the only permissible form of exchange between two dogs meeting for the first time will be the full length version of the ceremony most commonly known as 'Passing the Time of Day'. Even the most liberal minded Aquarian will have no time for the modern habit of cutting it short by skipping the preliminaries and rushing away before the finale.

The performance will begin at the first sighting—when

your dog sees another in the distance. The Aquarian will assume the haughty walk until he is near enough to waft the scent; a difficult movement as the only part of the body allowed to move is the very end of the nose which has to circle in an anti-clockwise direction until it has caught the full smell. This can take anything from one minute to five, depending on the direction and force of the wind.

This will be followed by a period of identification by sight when the Aquarian moves closer with the ritualistic stiff-legged walk and studies the other dog from all angles several times. By this time the strange dog will be thoroughly un-nerved and, when the Aquarian closes in for the final stages, will assume that he is about to be murdered in cold blood and leap to the attack. If the Aquarian has the advantage of size and weight it will not take him long to recover his guard and pin the other dog down to resume his investigations.

However, if, as is far more likely, your dog has picked a dog twice his size the result will not be so happy. In time you will come to accept finding a battered and blood-stained dog on your doorstep after unaccompanied trips outside the garden. There will be nothing that you can do about it as he would far rather be savaged than seen displaying bad manners. Walking past a strange dog without acknowledging it would be as unforgivable to him as forgetting to inquire into the health of each individual relation would be to an Arab.

AMOROUS INCLINATIONS

Sex will be a problem to both the male and female Aquarian. When young they will be too inhibited to advance a relation-ship beyond the stage of friendship, and when they do get old enough to overcome this they will not stay with any one dog for more than a few days. Short affairs that will not give.

them any extra responsibilities will suit them both; especially the bitch, as she will have no time for puppies.

The whole business will be something of a puzzle to them, and many Aquarians will not have any time for members of the opposite sex.

PHYSICAL CHARACTERISTICS

The Aquarian will be as slow and deliberate in his movement as he is in his thought. He will take as long to cross a room as a tortoise would to cross a road, and will hardly ever be persuaded into a run. He will be well built, slightly tall for his breed with deep set, wide apart eyes. He will be most easily recognised by the way that he holds his head—letting it droop and giving the impression that the thoughts inside it are too heavy for him to carry any farther.

The fact that he will always be loth to hurry himself will be the most likely cause of ill health. Aquarius is said to rule the blood, and bad circulation will give him perpetually cold extremities. The only cure will be exercise, faster and farther than is usual.

JUST YOUR BAD LUCK

This primitive Aquarian will be incapable of making up his mind for himself and will make an issue out of the most insignificant matters. He will have no concentration, no tact and no imagination. He will be unreliable, selfish and egotistical, so lacking in intelligence that at times he will give the impression that he suffers from mental deficiency.

Pisces

February 20 to March 20

The sign of the Duplicator or Interpreter
A mutable watery sign
Gentle, kind, retiring, unlucky and melancholy

Ruler: Neptune

Harmonious signs: Cancer, Scorpio, Virgo

Pisces

BASIC TEMPERAMENT

THIS is the strongest of the double signs. Tradition shows Pisces as two fishes, one struggling upstream, against the current while the other relaxes swimming downstream. The Piscean will differ in only one way from this: instead of having two forms, he will have both these opposing forces confined within one not very intelligent body.

He will be unpredictable from one minute to the next, torn between these two extremes as they take their turns at living. His life will be an ebb and flow of moodiness, changeability and contrariness as he is pulled and pushed by his innermost feelings. A dog that will not know whether he is coming or going, or if he has been.

Take a Piscean out for a walk and he will inevitably set off in the opposite direction to the one you had intended, but by the time you have decided to go along with him, he will have decided to go your way after all. He will be hungry and by the time you offer him food, replete. He will be all over you one minute—you will be in the dog-house the next. He will be equally contrary with your friends, treating one person like a long lost uncle on one visit and a dog thief the next time they call.

At least half of the time he will be a difficult dog and an anxiety to his owners. But like all Jekyll and Hydes he will have a good side to make up for some of the bad. After a spell of rubbing you up the wrong way he will be sweetness itself, for a little while.

But deep down inside himself, quite out of reach and beyond his control, he will be a good dog who intends to please rather than annoy. He will not wilfully mean to upset you, anger you or bring you to such a pitch that you throw things at him. Any harm he does do to those around him will have been caused inadvertently, which is always nice to know.

LEBENSRAUM

Pisces is ruled by Neptune and all Pisceans will have a close affinity to water and all that is wet, whether it be sea, river, rain or bath. Ideally this dog would like to live on a houseboat where he could enjoy the quiet and lapping water. Abandoned on dry land and made to live in an ordinary house he will do as much as he can to remedy the situation by making the most of any wet that happens to be to paw.

With his theme-song water, water everywhere, the Piscean would be able to find an oasis in the middle of an uncharted desert; he will revel in the shallowest puddle, rolling and splashing in the pure ecstasy of the feel of water on his skin. Country walks will turn into swimming galas as he shows his prowess in the art of dog-stroke, back-flips and deep water fishing. And when he has finished he will be sure that it is only out of deference to his supremacy in the water that you stayed on the bank. Knowing that you like water as much as he does, he will leap out and shake himself, spraying you with unselfish abandon.

If you live in a country district where the water belongs to a fishing syndicate, no amount of explaining will bring this fact within the Piscean's powers of comprehension. The only thing to do will be to tell the irate fishermen who come knocking at your door to explain it to the dog themselves. And if that does not work you can always claim that he is nothing to do with you and belongs to the people next door.

Rain will cause this dog as much excitement as heroin does to a narcotic. He will be driven to ecstacies of enjoyment as he frolics in the garden trying to catch each drop in his mouth. Then he will dash inside, bringing as much as he can with him, to show you what an improvement it is to your carpets and polished floors.

But there is one aspect of all this that can be a blessing in a dog: you will never have any trouble when it comes to bathing him. Pisceans have been known to sit in an empty bath waiting, and one even learnt to turn on the taps—although he could not make up his mind whether he preferred the hot or the cold.

When not playing at water-babies the Piscean will be exceedingly restless in the house, moving from room to room and occupation to occupation. Then just when your hair is standing on end and you are reaching out for the aspirin—

to send him to sleep as well as to sooth your nerves—he will stop and drift in to a coma-like state. Solitude and day dreaming will be a very important part of his life and when these fits occur he should be left undisturbed in the hope that they will last as long as possible.

SOCIAL INTEGRATION

Half the Piscean's life will be spent making things difficult for himself while the other half will be concerned with putting things right and smoothing ruffled feelings. He will be forceful and pushing until he has put everybody off and then he will be so gentle and retiring that you cannot help but love him.

If you noted the length and frequency of these two selfs, the good side would have been on view more than the other,

but you will never be able to count on this being so. You may congratulate yourself on him having a 'good day' when you are going to visit Aunt Maud, and decide to take him with you. By the time you get there, though, he will be well into a 'bad day' and you will have to control an unsociable dog that should never have been taken beyond the confines of your home.

But the Piscean will be easier to get along with than he sounds through a natural understanding of his position in the world. He will know, without you having to beat it into him, the role of a dog in a house. He will accept that he is only a small part of a whole and that if he wants his food and a roof over his head he will have to make the best of it.

Cancerians and Scorpionians are the most compatible people for the Piscean to live with. The Cancerian's sense of humour and his likelihood of making a success of his own life will mean that he will be able to give the Piscean the material security he needs: a yacht or oil-rig. While the Scorpionian will have enough devotion to overlook any amount of contrariness in his dog.

Arians also stand a good chance of living, if not in complete harmony, with a certain amount of success when close to a Piscean all day. But whatever your type, providing you have patience the Piscean will at least be easy to handle from the point of view that he will be indifferent to rules and regulations providing that complying with them will keep him out of Battersea Dogs' Home.

PERSONAL RELATIONSHIPS

Insults and assaults from other dogs will cause the Piscean to stop and think. He will never be a dog who leaps into an unpremeditated attack or rushes around looking for trouble. This disinclination to fight back or defend himself will mean that other dogs frequently get the chance to take advantage of him—which piece of news will quickly cover the neighbourhood. His sorties into the outside world will be full of hazards as unsociably-minded dogs leap out on him from behind telephone kiosks.

Eventually he may become so thwarted that you will find it impossible to get him out of the house unless you offer him protection in the form of yourself and a very large stick. You could try sending him to dog classes but very few of them have lessons in combat, unarmed or otherwise. You may have to accept the fact that yours is the perpetual underdog when in the presence of his own kind and sex, and pander to his whims by not forcing him out unless he is on the lead. You will also have to promise to carry him past all likely-looking places of ambush.

AMOROUS INCLINATIONS

The Piscean will have a strong romantic streak, but no sense whatsoever of loyalty or prolonged affection. He will be subject to strange adorations which will verge on hero-worship, and they will usually be for the most unlikely objects. It will not be beyond his capacity to fall in love with a cat which could prove embarrassing if the cat does not belong to you and he makes a habit of showing how he feels in someone elses garden.

Through his fickle nature you will always be meeting new people. The Piscean is a wonderful way of breaking the ice when you move to a new area—it will only take him a few days to have all the owners of female dogs on their way to pay you a call. But they will never have time to get really nasty for his whistle-stop visits will be over almost before they have begun.

PHYSICAL CHARACTERISTICS

The Piscean will be of insignificant appearance without any outstanding physical characteristics. He will be the kind of dog you would not look at twice unless he happens to be yours when you will have no choice as it is impossible to turn a blind eye the whole time.

He will be active and enjoy playing games and unfortunately prone to leg and foot trouble. If it is not a torn ligament from slipping on the soap in the bath, it will be ingrowing toenails.

It will be a help if you can get your dog used to having his toenails clipped while he is still small enough for you to pin down with one arm. The other hand will then be free to perform the delicate operation, and you will be less likely to hurt him. Then, by the time he is fully grown and they start in earnest, he will be so used to the performance that you will be able to do it with your eyes shut instead of having to hold him over the gas to send him to sleep.

JUST YOUR BAD LUCK

The primitive Piscean will be the eternal coming and going, running and jumping dog. He will drift through life with no purpose other than to change his mind and mood more times than any one dog has done before. The fact that he can change from an amiable, playful pet into a miserable anti-social beast at the mere flick of an eye-lid will enchant him, and he will repeat the trick again—and again.

He will crave excessive comforts. Hot-water bottles at night, meals in bed and sugar in his early morning tea. He will not dream of lying on the grass unless you spread a rug out for him first.

Any form of emotional outlet will be leapt at and played to the full. And if you try to keep everything on an even pitch he will resort to helping himself to artificial stimulants—yeast tablets and purple hearts—to achieve the same effect. He will have no sense of ownership for other people's belongings being a firm believer that finders is keepers.